MS. AMERICAN DREAM

ALSO BY PATRICIA WILLIAMS-LEE

Rabbit

MS. AMERICAN DREAM

A MEMOIR OF MAKING IT, NO MATTER WHAT

PATRICIA WILLIAMS-LEE

WITH JEANNINE AMBER

ATRIA BOOKS

New York Amsterdam/Antwerp London
Toronto Sydney/Melbourne New Delhi

ATRIA BOOKS
An Imprint of Simon & Schuster, LLC
1230 Avenue of the Americas
New York, NY 10020

The authorized representative in the EEA is Simon & Schuster Nederland B.V., Herculesplein 96, 3584 AA Utrecht, Netherlands. info@simonandschuster.nl

First Atria Books hardcover edition September 2026

Some names and identifying characteristics have been changed.

Interior design by Davina Mock-Maniscalco

Manufactured in the United States of America

1 3 5 7 9 10 8 6 4 2

Library of Congress Control Number: 2026938994

ISBN 978-1-6680-4421-6
ISBN 978-1-6680-4423-0 (ebook)

For my family,

thank you for letting me chase my dreams

When someone tells me no, that don't mean it's over.
It means I gotta find another way.

—Ms. Pat

MS. AMERICAN DREAM

CHAPTER 1

A DIFFERENT WORLD

The summer after second grade, I learned three important lessons that would shape me for the rest of my life. Back then, I lived with my mama, Mildred, my sister, Sweetie, and our three brothers in a run-down one-bedroom duplex on Griffin Street on the south side of Atlanta. The neighborhood was filled with hardworking poor folks and people on public assistance, like my mama.

Most kids I knew spent their days at the YMCA rec center on Butler Street. It had a summer program with all kinds of fun activities, like basketball, kickball, and double Dutch competitions. For snacks, everybody got Little Hugs juice boxes and little bags of chips. I would have gone to the Y just for that.

The cost of the summer program was on a sliding scale based on income, which meant Mildred could have sent me for free. But when I gave her forms to fill out, she waved me away like I was handing her a stack of bills she couldn't pay. Mama and I was having this conversation in the living room, which was also Mama's bedroom. She slept on a ratty old sofa. Me and my sister had the bedroom. Our brothers, when they were home, stayed in a little room off the kitchen that didn't even have a door.

"Get that shit out my face," Mildred said, taking a slow drag off her Winston. "And why you lookin' at me? Bitch, you better fix your face and fix me a drink." I don't know if she was too lazy to fill out the paperwork, or if the problem was that she didn't know how to read. Maybe she was ornery that morning because she hadn't had her breakfast gin. Whatever the reason, my mama didn't sign me up for the YMCA, which meant I had nothing to do on those long, hot summer days. I sure as hell wasn't trying to stay home with my mama. That's why I started sneaking out of the house.

One thing about Mildred: she watched TV like it was her full-time job. Starting at eleven in the morning when *The Price Is Right* came on, she'd sit there, eyeballs glued to the set, until damn near four in the afternoon when the credits rolled at the end of *Guiding Light*. She was so mesmerized by her stories and her liquor that she didn't even notice her youngest child was missing.

The first time I took off, I didn't tell nobody I was leaving. It was the middle of the day, and the house was hot as hell. My brother Andre and my sister Sweetie were in the kitchen, making all kinds of racket arguing over which one of them would get the last slice of the bread to make a sugar sandwich. *I'm sick of this shit*, I thought to myself.

I went out to the yard, picked up an old rickety chair that was lying upside down in the bushes, and pulled it up to the side of the house. I went back inside, checked to make sure the bedroom was empty, then climbed out the window, stepping onto the chair. I jumped my little ass into the yard, and just like Dr. Martin Luther King Jr. said, Thank God Almighty, I was free at last!

I was gone all day and into the night. It felt so good to be out on my own, the next day I did it again. Pretty soon, sneaking out of the house became my daily routine.

When I took off, I never had a plan or particular place to go. I'd just walk up and down and all around the neighborhood. I'd pass the corner store where my brothers stole cans of Vienna sausages when we was hungry, and the convenience store where the owner would let folks buy stuff on credit. Every month Mildred would run up her tab buying Winstons and Schlitz Malt Liquor Bull, then pay the owner with her food stamps when they came in.

Mildred had a lot of problems: she was broke, unemployed, uneducated, and addicted to alcohol. But her worst quality was her mean-ass fiery temper. If I did any little thing wrong—like taking too long to light her cigarette off the hot plate—she'd lose her fucking mind. "You got an ass whooping on the shelf!" she'd holler, which meant if she caught me messing up again, she'd beat my ass until the switch was as thin as a pencil.

One morning, a couple of weeks after I started sneaking out of the house, Mama hollered from the living room that I needed to go fix her a drink. Her beverage of choice was Seagram's Extra Dry Gin—which we called Bumpy Face, after the texture on the bottle—and tap water. Only, I wasn't no damn bartender. I was an eight-year-old trying to keep her mama from getting bent. So when I mixed her drink, I went heavy on the water and light on the booze. She should have thanked me for keeping her hydrated. Instead, Mildred hit the roof.

"Girl, why you fuck up my drink like this?" she yelled. "You know it's equal water to equal gin. Get me a switch—that ass whooping coming right off the shelf now."

That night, I lay awake with my ass on fire and hatred in my heart. I thought long and hard until I came up with a plan to solve all my problems. The next day when I climbed out the bedroom window, I decided I wasn't never coming back.

My big idea was to go stay by my daddy. I barely knew the man. He'd walked out on the family when I was still a baby. And I'd only been to his place a couple of times, when Mama, drunk as a skunk, dragged me over there then made me sit on the stoop while she banged on his door and screamed that he wasn't nothing but a low-down dirty dog. I wasn't even sure I remembered what he looked like (I pictured a cross between Lamont Sanford from *Sanford and Son* and James Evans from *Good Times*). But none of that mattered, because I'd watched enough television to know that my plan would surely work.

On TV, daddies love and protect their kids, and they enjoy having them around. Even that shriveled-up old white dude on *Diff'rent Strokes* loved those two little Black boys he adopted. If a father's love was powerful enough to bond different races, I reckoned my daddy would be more than happy to take me in.

That morning, I gathered up two pairs of pants, some underwear, and two T-shirts—my entire wardrobe—to take with me. I couldn't find a bag to carry them in, so I just threw everything out the window before climbing out myself. I picked my clothes off the yard, scrunched them into a ball, then marched my little ass, with all my worldly possessions, to the bus stop around the corner.

I paid the fare with loose change I stole from my brother Dre's pocket, rode for a while, and got off at the stop where I remembered Mama taking me. Then I walked up one block and down another until I found a wood frame house with a yellow door that looked like the one Mama banged on when she had her screaming fits on Daddy's porch.

It was high noon and all I wanted was a cool drink and something to put in my empty belly. But my daddy, who had a job in construction, was still at work. For hours, I sat on the front stoop waiting on him and daydreaming about my wonderful new life. The longer I sat, the better my fantasy got. In my imagination, my daddy was not only going to rescue me from my mama's bullshit but he was also going to tell me nice things every morning, like, "Don't you look pretty today!"

I was hungry and thirsty and halfway to a heatstroke when I saw my daddy walking towards the house. He was bigger than I remembered, dressed in dusty jeans and work boots. His forehead was dripping sweat. When he noticed me waiting for him, he stopped dead in his tracks.

"Hey," he said.

"Hey," I said back.

For a while, the two of us just looked at each other in silence. Finally, he asked, "Yo' mama know you here?"

"Yes, sir," I lied. "She told me to come."

"Huh," he said, scratching his head. "Well, shoot, I guess you might as well come on in." He opened the door, and I followed him into his tidy one-bedroom apartment. When he disappeared into the bathroom to shower off the day, I got busy inspecting my new accommodations.

My daddy, I discovered, was living a life of luxury. He had food in the fridge, electric and gas turned on, and hot water flowing from the faucet. At home, Mildred was always behind on the bills, so we never had all those things at once. She kept the lights on so people outside couldn't see we was struggling, but inside, the stove didn't work. She used a hot plate to boil water and cook food, when she had it.

My favorite thing about Daddy's place was how peaceful it was. Compared to the chaos and commotion I was used to, his home felt like the quietest place on earth.

He gave me a bowl of spaghetti and a clean pillow and told me I could sleep on the sofa. The next morning, he said, "Don't touch nothing." Then he left for work. With no one to bother me, I had the most relaxing day of my life. I turned on the TV and watched *The Price Is Right* and *The Young and the Restless*; I went outside to sit on the porch and watch people go by. I fried up some bacon for breakfast and made myself a bologna sandwich for lunch. Before Daddy came home, I cleaned all the dishes and put them away. The next morning when he left for work, I had the same excellent day as the one before.

I thought things were going pretty good. But it seemed my daddy felt different. On Saturday morning, after I'd been sleeping on his sofa for almost a week, he woke up and came into the living room, scratching his belly.

"You still here?" he asked.

I nodded.

He shook his head and turned to walk away. Then he paused, as if having a second thought, and swiveled back to face me. "This ain't gon' work," he said. "You can't stay here no more."

"How come?" I asked, confused.

"I'm paying yo' mama child support," he said. "You gon' mess up her money. I gotta take you back." I knew he was lying. That man ain't never gave Mildred a single penny. He was just looking for excuses to hide the fact that he was a deadbeat daddy kicking his own baby girl to the curb.

I didn't try to argue. In fact, I didn't say nothing at all. I put on my stone face to let my daddy know that if he didn't want me, I didn't even care. On the way back to Mildred's, I stared out the passenger-side window fighting back tears, clutching my tangled ball of clothes to my chest. I couldn't believe the man I'd thought would protect me was driving me right back to the gates of hell.

My daddy was no James Evans or Mr. Drummond. His ass wasn't any better than my mama. I realized then that I had exactly zero people in the world to count on. No one was going to save me from the bullshit. If I wanted a better life, I needed to figure it out on my own.

That was lesson number one.

Looking back on that summer, I can't believe how damn negligent both my parents were. My daddy was way out of order for taking me back to live with my abusive, alcoholic mama. But Mildred was even worse for paying me so little attention that she didn't even know I was sneaking out the house. Letting your eight-year-old daughter roam free is bad behavior for any mother at any time. But this was 1980. There was a killer on the loose, and children like me were the targets.

Between 1979 and 1981, more than two dozen Black folks, most of them children and teens, were murdered in Atlanta. Twelve-year-old Angel Lenair was found dead in a wooded lot on Campbellton Road, not far from where I lived. The killer had bound Angel's hands with an electric cord and stuffed a pair of underwear in her mouth. Angel was his fifth victim. The body of his twentieth victim, Curtis Walker, was found floating in the Chattahoochee River. Curtis Walker was my cousin, on my mama's side. The Atlanta Child Murders hit that close to home.

Folks could see the police weren't doing enough to keep us safe. Black mothers were terrified and kept their children close. But not Mildred. Most nights, she'd only discover I was missing after I got picked up and brought home by the police. They'd tell her to be careful having a little girl out past curfew. She'd smile her no-teeth-having grin and thank the officers for their trouble. But the second they were gone, she'd beat the dog shit outta me for bringing police to her door.

I wasn't scared of the beatings, the cops, *or* Mama's temper. The next day, I'd go right back to climbing out the window, again.

That summer, like every summer in Atlanta, was sticky and humid and miserable as hell. It wasn't no walking-around-type weather. So one afternoon, sweaty and worn-out, and with my flip-flops so thin they was melting on the pavement, I decided to get on the bus that stopped near the corner of Griffin Street and Simpson Road.

This time, I didn't have a dime, a nickel, or even a penny for the fare. But I smiled at the driver and asked him for a ride. He looked me up and down, nodded his head, and told me to take a seat. I stayed on that bus for hours, riding his route back and forth, with my face pressed against the window. The farther we got from where I lived, the nicer the neighborhoods became.

We drove through Vine City and into Dixie Hills. The houses weren't big and fancy, but I noticed little things, like the way I didn't see no busted-up refrigerators sitting on anybody's front porch or broke down hoopties with mismatched doors parked at the curb. Instead, I saw houses with tidy yards, clean windows, and pretty matching curtains. At home, Mildred covered her windows with bedsheets that were faded and torn.

The first time we passed through Dixie Hills, I saw a mama in a flowered housecoat sweeping dust off her porch and a man in a T-shirt mowing his lawn with a cigarette hanging out the side of his mouth. The second time we drove through the neighborhood, I saw a whole happy-ass family on what looked like an afternoon stroll. The mama was pushing a baby stroller. The daddy was holding hands with a little kid. But what really got me was the way the parents were laughing and talking together, both of them wearing cheese-eating grins. The only other time I saw Black folks looking so jolly was in McDonald's commercials.

Around five thirty in the afternoon, the Bus Driver said it was time for his lunch break. "You hungry?" he asked, glancing my way.

"Yes, sir," I said. "I sure could eat something right about now."

He stopped the bus, ran into a quick mart, then drove around the corner to a quiet street, where he pulled over and parked the bus. He took out his silver lunch pail and offered me half of his bologna sandwich. Then he handed me the can of apple juice, bag of cheese curls, and Little Debbie oatmeal pie he'd picked up at the store. I enjoyed the hell outta that lunch. But I liked the conversation even more.

The Bus Driver wasn't anything like grown folks I was used to.

He didn't get mad when I asked him questions. Not one time did he tell me to shut the fuck up.

"How many kids you got?" I asked.

"Three."

"What they names?"

"Frederick, Franny, and Fabian."

"*Fabian*? What kinda name is that?"

He sighed. "My wife picked it out."

"How many baby mamas you got?"

"Just the one."

"You ever seen *The Young and the Restless*?"

He chuckled. "I don't reckon I have."

I had a real good time with the Bus Driver. When he dropped me off at the end of his shift, I asked, "Can I ride with you tomorrow?"

"You sure can, little lady," he replied. The next day, I spent all afternoon keeping him company. By my third day riding his route, me and the Bus Driver were best friends.

I liked the way he asked me questions and always seemed interested in what I had to say. Sometimes he'd act real goofy just to make me laugh. He had a little transistor radio he kept in the front pocket of his jacket. When the route was slow, and it was just a couple of people on the bus, he'd turn up the music and sing along as he drove.

"*Ain't no mountain high enough*," he belted one day. "Now, you can't tell me I don't sound just like Miss Diana Ross," he said, winking at me in the rearview mirror. I laughed my head off and told him he sure as heck did not.

The Bus Driver worked from two in the afternoon until ten at night. When his lunch break came, at five thirty sharp, he always asked if I was hungry. And he always had something for me to eat. At first, he'd share whatever he was having. Then one day, he shocked the shit outta me by reaching into his lunch box and handing me a brown paper bag. Inside was my very own bologna, lettuce, and tomato sandwich, carefully wrapped in wax paper, plus a little-kid juice box, a bag of Lay's potato chips, and a snack box of Sunkist raisins.

"You made this for me?" I asked, smiling so big I thought my face might crack open.

"My wife did," he said. "She thinks you keeping me outta trouble. She told me to tell you, 'Hello.'"

I don't know what that Bus Driver told his wife, but that lady fed me *real* good. She made all types of sandwiches: tuna salad, peanut butter and jelly, and ham and cheese. Sometimes, she sent cut-up carrot sticks or half an apple. One time, I reached into my paper bag and found two Oreo cookies wrapped in a paper towel. "Your wife's real nice," I told the Bus Driver. "I never had no lunches this good before."

"I'm glad you're enjoying yourself," he said. For me, those sandwiches were more than just a treat. When Mama's food stamps ran out at the end of the month, sometimes that lunch I had with the Bus Driver was the only food I'd eat all day.

Every afternoon during his break, we'd sit on that empty bus eating and chopping it up like a couple of lifelong friends. I learned he had a pet dog named Bo and his favorite hobby was fishing. I told him my mama drank too damn much and that the kids at my school were mean as hell to me. "I don't like none of them hoes," I shared one day.

He raised his eyebrows. "So what *do* you like?"

"I like riding the bus with you."

He smiled.

"And I like my teacher," I added. "She's bad to the bone."

I told him about the big-ass globe my second-grade teacher kept on top of her desk. "You ever seen a globe before?" I asked. "My teacher says all them different shapes is different countries. You ever been to any of those places? Like China or Africa? They look so far away."

The Bus Driver said one time that he and his wife went to Florida for a vacation. "But we saving up for someplace special," he added. "My wife wants to go to Egypt to see the ancient pyramids. When you grow up, you can visit all kinds of places, too."

"I already seen all kinds of different things."

"That right?"

"Every day, riding your bus."

"See how God works," he said, chuckling. "You didn't even have to travel that far to see something new in this world."

Before that summer, I thought that all of Atlanta was like my broke-down neighborhood, and that the only way I would ever see something different was to visit one of the countries my second-grade teacher showed me on her globe. The Bus Driver showed me that another kind of life—one with clean curtains, happy families, and tidy front yards—was possible not that far from home.

That was lesson number two.

It's a miracle I survived that summer. I could have been another murdered child. Or stepped onto a different bus and met a child-predator instead.

For a girl with no supervision, the world is a dangerous place. At that young age, I'd already seen plenty of evil up close. I'd been beaten, molested, and neglected. My own mama treated me worse than a stray dog. Maybe God sent me the Bus Driver to show me what kindness feels like. The Bus Driver gave me shelter, kept me safe, and fed me when I was hungry. He never asked for anything in return.

That summer I learned that the devil isn't always trying to get at you. Sometimes, God will send you an angel instead.

That was lesson number three.

CHAPTER 2

"THE AMERICAN DREAM AIN'T FOR US"

When I was twenty-one years old, I got a job working as a medical assistant in a doctor's office about a forty-minute drive from where I grew up. I'd gotten the job through the state of Georgia's Welfare-to-Work program, which was supposed to help folks like me get off public assistance. In my case, becoming a medical assistant was part of a bigger plan: I was trying to turn my life around.

Making a change was my husband Michael's idea. When we met, I was a hustler, selling drugs and forging checks. But Michael is a hardworking, law-abiding, ex-military man. He didn't want no criminal-minded woman. He wanted me to stop chasing fast cash and start living on the right side of the law.

At first, I tried to argue. I told him it would take damn near three months at a regular job for me to earn what I made in a single night selling crack. "And I don't like working for other people," I added. "I like running things. That's why I'm a small-business owner."

"You can call it whatever you want," Michael said. "But that don't make it legal. And it don't make it right."

We went back and forth for weeks. Michael kept saying that life wasn't just about making money. He said I also needed to think about the kids. The two of us were raising six children by then. I had a son and a daughter from my deadbeat baby daddy; we also had my sister's four girls. We took them in because my sister was down bad, deep in a love affair with crack. "None of the kids have my last name," Michael said. "If you end up in jail, they all might end up in the system. Is that really what you want?"

Sometimes Michael gets on my nerves with his love of doing things the right way. He's the type to read the instruction manual cover to cover before he plugs in a new toaster. I hate how careful and cautious he is. But when it came to the children, deep down I knew he was right. So, I gave up my life of crime, went through the Welfare-to-Work program, got my GED, signed up for medical assistant training, and got myself a legal job.

Every morning, I put on my blue scrubs, smiled at the patients, and asked how they were feeling. I took temperatures, checked blood pressure, and recorded patients' information in the doctor's charts. I didn't mind the work. I liked helping people. But compared to my previous lifestyle, filling out workers' comp forms was about as boring as it gets.

It was a job, not a passion. I almost never thought about the patients after I clocked out for the day and went home. Until I met the Trucker.

It was early October—the leaves on the oak tree out front had just started changing color—when the Trucker walked through the clinic's door. He was nice-looking, big and beefy like my husband, and dressed in blue jeans, steel-toe boots, and a collared work shirt.

I took him to an exam room and asked the reason for his visit.

"Brown recluse spider got me," he said. "That sombitch musta crawled right up my pants leg." He pointed to a spot on his right upper thigh. When I placed my hand on the wound, sure enough it felt hot and inflamed.

"Good thing you came in," I said. "That spider got you good."

I took his vitals and medical history and asked about his job. He told me he worked as a long-haul trucker. "Been from one side of the country to the other," he said. "Different cities, same bullshit no matter where you is."

I looked up from my notes and caught the Trucker staring at a button I'd pinned to the front of my scrubs, a picture of my son Nikia in his baseball uniform, grinning from ear to ear.

"That your boy?" he asked. "You just got the one?"

"I got six at home," I told him.

He let out a slow whistle. "I hope you married," he said. "You gotta do right by them Black kids."

"I know that's right," I said politely. I thought this would be the end of the chitchat portion of the appointment. But apparently, the Trucker thought a young mother like me needed to hear his wisdom. Because just as I was turning to go check on the next patient, he leaned forward as though he were going to tell me a secret. "Miss," he hissed. "You gotta be careful."

"Careful about what?"

"The white man," he answered. "They been feeding us a pack of lies." He paused, darting his eyes around the exam room like he was checking for hidden cameras. "You heard about the American dream, right?" he continued. "They gon' teach you it's for *everybody*. But really, it ain't for no people who been brought here in chains. That lie is how they keep the Black man in bondage. That's the whole plan right there."

The Trucker sounded just like my granddaddy. Before he got locked up for attempted murder, Granddaddy loved yelling at Walter Cronkite as he delivered the evening news. "Look how them crackers is doing us now!" Granddaddy hollered one night. "These white devils out there in Boston throwing rocks at a bus full of babies just tryna go to school. Every damn one of them rotten to the core." I was too young to understand what Granddaddy was watching. But I remember his anger. The Trucker had that same fire.

"Let me break it down for you," he continued. "Prime example: You see how niggas be out here scrambling to get them a big house with a backyard and a pet dog and a wife and all that. You ever wonder why that is?" He looked at me like he was waiting for an answer.

"Don't everybody want a nice house?" I asked.

"Exactly!" he said, raising a finger in the air. "That's the brainwashing right there. Everybody wants a house because it's a *signifier*. It's a symbol of success. But what *really* happens is we buy a house, then we become slaves to the bank. For thirty years, you got a mortgage keeping you in shackles." He held his wrists together like he was locked in invisible handcuffs. "You feel me?" he asked. "Shackles," he repeated. "Just like they did our ancestors."

I didn't know much about real estate, but I was pretty sure owning a home wasn't as bad as slavery. But I kept smiling and nodding, because I wasn't supposed to argue with the patients. I already got yelled at by the office manager for listing a patient's race as "clear" instead of "white" on that patient's chart.

The Trucker must have sensed I needed more convincing, because he just kept right on talking. "The American dream ain't for us," he repeated. "That shit ain't nothing but a lie. While we busy saving dollars for our little house and yard, the white man is busy buying up McDonald's franchises. Why? So they have a *legacy* to pass down to they children!" To emphasize his point, he slapped his big-ass palm on the exam table so hard it made me jump. "They setting they kids up for easy street and investing in they future."

For the first time since he started yapping, I was getting interested. I wanted to hear more about these "franchises" and "legacies" and how I could get something to pass down to *my* kids.

Growing up, I never heard nobody talking about the future. The closest anybody got to financial planning was when Mildred talked about winning the lotto. Her big plan was to buy every living room suite, luxury vehicle, and thirty-six-inch color Zenith she saw on *The Price Is Right*. "Just as soon as my number hit," she'd say. "I'm buying up *all* that shit."

I had so many questions for the Trucker. But I never got the chance to ask. Just then, the door opened, and the doctor walked in. "That'll be all, Patricia," he said. He took my clipboard from my hands without even looking me in the eye.

The Trucker leaned forward and hissed a last warning in my direction: "Girl, don't believe the hype."

For weeks, I couldn't get the Trucker's words out of my head. He spoke with such conviction, it sounded like he was making sense. But the words he was saying were the opposite of everything I believed. He said Black homeowners had been lied to, trapped, and brainwashed. But I wanted to be a homeowner more than anything in the world.

When I was little, every time Mildred fell behind on rent, we'd have to throw all our stuff into trash bags and vacate the premises before the eviction notice got nailed to the door. I must have lived in a dozen different places by my tenth birthday. Anytime I got comfortable, we'd suddenly have to split. I wanted my kids to have the safety, security, and stability I didn't have growing up. That meant I needed to have a place they could always come back to, no matter how bad the world was outside our doors.

Owning a home was my goal in life. For a long time, I couldn't square the Trucker's words with my feelings on the matter. Then one day, it hit me: The Trucker had it only *halfway* right. It's not chasing the American dream that'll mess you up. It's the scammers, schemers, and hustlers who try to trick and trap you along the way.

CHAPTER 3

FRAUDULENT BEHAVIOR

A couple of years before I met the Trucker, I was living in a three-bedroom apartment near Greenbriar Mall with Michael and my two kids. I was proud as hell of that place because it was filled with all kinds of shit. I had a leather white-on-white living room suite, a home entertainment system with a laser disc player, and closets overflowing with clothes. In my bedroom, I had a queen-size waterbed because back then we thought that shit was sexy. I paid for all my possessions with money I made selling drugs.

When I started my business, I was a fifteen-year-old single mama, trying to make enough to feed my two kids. Back then, I didn't understand the power of addiction. I thought smoking crack was a lifestyle choice and that crackheads could stop if they really wanted. I only learned that crack could take over your body and mind when I started seeing my customers lose everything—their jobs, families, and all their small appliances—trying to chase that high.

I met my customer Elroy when he bought a dime bag from me one Friday night on his way home from work. He was clean-cut and nice-looking, wearing a white button-down shirt and a navy jacket with a MARTA logo, the same uniform the Bus Driver wore. At first,

Elroy was a casual user, hitting me up for a dime bag or two on the weekend. Then he started buying on weeknights. Then early mornings on his way to work, too. Before long, Elroy lost his job. One night, he tried to sell me a brand-new baby's car seat for a couple of rocks.

"C'mon, girl, do me a solid," he begged.

I saw how easy it was for dope fiends' lives to come undone. But when my sister almost lost her kids behind her addiction, it became a different kind of real to me.

I hadn't talked to Sweetie in almost a year. Then one night she called screaming into the phone that Child Protective Services was at her door, trying to take her kids. I dropped everything and rushed right over. Her place was so filthy, the roaches would walk up and shake your hand. The living room was littered with trash and broken furniture. There were overflowing ashtrays in every corner and empty soda cans rolling around the floor. Down the hall, the bathroom toilet was backed up with the bowl full to the rim.

Sweetie was twitching and tweaking and talking to herself about how she's *not* no unfit mama, and she *loves* her babies, and this was all some *fuck-ass bullshit*, and she just needs a few days to get back on her feet. As she spoke, she kept trying to light the wrong side of a Newport with a broken Bic lighter. "Rabbit," she said, calling me by my childhood nickname, "you know this shit ain't right."

When we were younger, Sweetie was the pretty one. I'd been cursed with real bad acne and a Jheri curl that was always dried-out and crispy. Meanwhile, Sweetie looked like the model on the Dark and Lovely box. By the time she was twenty years old, the drugs had taken all that pretty away. Now she was just like every other crackhead, with nappy hair, ashy skin, and wearing faded biker shorts that once upon a time had been neon pink. But it was the sight of her children that broke my heart most of all. Those four little girls—the ones the caseworker told me "needed to be removed from the home for their own safety"—were the most pitiful, uncared-for children I'd ever seen. The oldest, LaDontay, was eight. Her sister Diamond was five, and the two little ones, Destiny and Jonelle, were still in diapers. All of them were underfed, unwashed, and covered in ringworm. And they was *funky* as all hell.

I was only nineteen and not ready to be a mama of six. But if I didn't take them, the caseworker would. Then they'd all end up in the system. I took the girls back to my apartment that night. I washed and combed their hair, clipped their nails, and cleaned behind their ears. They went to bed smelling like Johnson's baby powder and pink baby lotion.

Me and Michael had been together less than a year when I brought my four nieces home to live with us. Most men would walk out on a situation like that. But I told him, "We the only family they got." I guess his soft heart melted. At twenty-one, Michael was a father to half a dozen little kids, and not one of them was his.

Taking in four extra babies is a big expense. That's why the government has assistance programs for people who step up and give children in crisis a loving home. I got food stamps to help feed them, Medicaid so I could take them to the doctor, and subsidized daycare so I could go out and work. But the biggest game changer was Section 8.

My apartment was already overflowing with toys and clothes. With four more girls, we needed more room. Sweetie's caseworker arranged for me to get a Section 8 housing voucher so we could afford a place big enough for a family of eight.

Me and Michael spent weeks looking at different rentals trying to find the perfect home. Some of the houses were in real bad neighborhoods, with drug dealers hanging out on the block. Back when I was hustling, I used to keep a .38 pistol in Nikia's diaper bag and hide a Ziploc baggie full of crack rocks in my daughter's drawers. But now that I was out of that life, I didn't want my children anywhere near that mess.

Finally, we found the perfect spot: a redbrick house in Riverdale, a quiet suburb outside Atlanta. The place looked okay from the outside, but inside it had slime-green carpet in the living room and cockroaches in the kitchen cabinets. It was the neighborhood—with its safe streets and good schools—that won us over. Even the landlord, a little old lady named Ms. Gertie, seemed nice. She was tiny, barely five feet tall, with a jacked-up hip that made her waddle like a duck. She smiled a lot and called me "dear."

The way Section 8 worked was that they calculated 30 percent of my gross income, minus deductions I got for each child I had in the house, and that was the amount I was expected to pay in rent. Ms. Gertie charged seven hundred and fifty dollars a month for that four-bedroom house. I was making minimum wage at McDonald's, five dollars and fifteen cents an hour. Minimum wage is supposed to be enough to live on. But anybody who's ever been paid minimum wage knows that's nothing but a joke. Thirty percent of my monthly income, after deductions, was thirty-nine dollars. That Section 8 voucher covered the rest.

The thing I liked most about Riverdale was its homey, peaceful vibe. Folks were always out in their yards waving hello to each other. I'd never seen this type of neighborliness before. I'd also never lived around these types of people. In Riverdale, it seemed like damn near everybody had a college education and a good-paying legal job.

Donna, who lived next door, worked as a middle school teacher; her husband had a job with the city. Roxanne, from one street over, worked at Coca-Cola's corporate office downtown; her husband was at Delta Airlines. And not one of my neighbors had six kids in the house, like we did. They all had a regular amount of children, like two or three.

It was a whole new world. But I liked it. I wanted so badly to fit in.

Before we moved to Riverdale, I only knew two people who went to college: Brenda, who I met in Fulton County Jail, where I got locked up for selling drugs, and Lamont, my supplier back when I sold crack. Neither one of them ever said so to my face, but I got the feeling that both of them thought they were better than folks like me.

Lamont wasn't like drug dealers you see on TV. He wore eyeglasses and half-zip pullover sweaters. He always had a paperback novel shoved in the back pocket of his jeans. He was nice to me and never disrespectful. But I noticed that whenever he came over to drop off dope and collect his money, he always tried to educate and elevate my ass. He'd say things like, "What you need is to break free from the ghetto mentality." Then he'd take me to an upscale furniture store, a luxury car dealership, or a restaurant with cloth napkins to give me a taste of what he called "the better things in life." One time, he took me to Neiman Marcus to show me designer brands, like Louis Vuitton and Gucci.

"Now *this* is the type of shit you should like," he told me, stroking a two-hundred-dollar calfskin leather belt. I appreciated Lamont opening my eyes to new experiences. But it was obvious that he thought the best way for me to improve myself was to upgrade my tastes to match his.

Brenda never came right out and said she thought she was better than me, either. But she came pretty close. She was thirty-four years old, tall, with light skin and fake-ass titties that sat high on her chest. She looked like she just walked out of a music video. Sometimes Brenda said she got locked up for a traffic violation or a "misunderstanding." Other times, she claimed she was there for doing "white-collar crime."

Meanwhile, we all knew she got busted for passing bad checks at the mall. Everybody, including the guards, hated Brenda and her stuck-up attitude. But I thought it took a whole lot of nerve for her to act like she was too fancy for jail when her Black ass was behind bars.

During my incarceration, Brenda became one of my best jail friends. I liked her because she helped me write letters to Travis, the bony-ass nigga I was kissing on before I met Michael. Brenda knew a lot of big words.

One time, two girls was getting into it over a pack of Jumbo Honey Buns. They was yelling and cussing at the top of their lungs, going round and round about who stole what and when. Brenda just rolled her eyes. "At this point," she said, "it's getting redundant." I'd never heard that word before.

Redundant. Definition: repetitive; using more words than necessary. Translation: Y'all keep saying the exact same shit.

Brenda had the gift of gab. But she also talked a lot of bullshit, especially about girls she didn't like. She'd call them "ignorant," "undignified," or "uncouth." And I couldn't help but notice that all the girls she labeled "ghetto trash" were just regular, around-the-way hood chicks, which meant Brenda probably thought those same things about me.

It didn't seem to matter to Lamont or Brenda that they were living what some folks might call a degenerate low-class lifestyle. They still had that I'm-better-than-you mentality. I figured that type of attitude comes from being educated and middle class.

When me and Michael moved to Riverdale, I realized I was surrounded by people just like Brenda and Lamont. For the first time in my life, I felt self-conscious about who I was and where I came from. I didn't want my new neighbors judging me. I was even more worried that they'd look down on my kids. I decided quickly that the best way to protect myself and the kids was to fake the funk and do everything I could to look like we belonged.

The first thing I did was enroll the older kids in all kinds of after-school activities at the Riverdale Recreation Center, about fifteen minutes from the house. I signed Nikia up for football, baseball, and basketball. I put Ashley and my two oldest nieces, LaDontay and Diamond, in cheerleading. Destiny was just a toddler, and little Jonelle was only a few months old. On the weekends, I fixed Destiny's hair in little Afro puffs, put the two of them in a double stroller, and promenaded around the park.

When I was little, we didn't play in parks. The park was where folks drank, fucked, or got shot at. Instead, me and my sister would try to find things to do in the yard. At one place we lived, somebody had left an old yellow refrigerator on the porch. One afternoon, Sweetie and her friends thought it would be funny to shove me inside and take off running. I guess they forgot to come back. If my uncle hadn't passed by and heard me hollering, I would have suffocated for sure. In my neighborhood, the games we played could kill you. In Riverdale, my kids had nothing but clean, safe fun.

The rec center was great for the kids. It was even better for me. That's where I did all my important surveillance, listening in on my neighbors, trying to figure out what these people were all about.

One afternoon, not long after we moved in, I sat on the bleachers at the baseball field, watching Nikia run his little ass around the bases. But really, I was hard at work, listening to the mothers sitting on the bleacher behind me. They weren't talking about normal stuff like who got shot the night before. These women spent the entire first inning talking about flowers—petunias, marigolds, and begonias—they were planting in their front yards.

It sounded like, for them, gardening was more than a hobby. This felt like a competition. I wasn't trying to sit on the sidelines of the neighborhood gardening wars, so after the game, I went straight to Home Depot and bought a trowel, a bag of topsoil, and three dozen red clay bricks.

I'd never planted flowers before. Where I grew up, people put old recliners or broke-down hoopties out in their front yards. At one place, my mama used the yard like it was a damn kitchen. She'd fallen behind on the gas bill, and the stove didn't work, so she went out and bought one of them little charcoal barbecue grills. Then she got busy frying up some catfish in the yard. She was out there in her old housedress with a plastic shower cap over her Jheri curl where everybody—including kids I went to school with—could see. I was so embarrassed. She didn't even care.

I spent a whole weekend digging out that flower bed, edging it with bricks, and planting a whole mess of pink azaleas and purple petunias, all of them laid out just so. That was my first home beautification project. Then I discovered that my neighbors did this type of shit all year round.

A few months later, at Little League football practice, I overheard Roxanne tell my next-door neighbor Donna that she liked the autumn wreath Donna had hung on her door. "So festive!" Roxanne remarked.

When practice was over, I went straight to Walmart and bought a big-ass circle covered with red and yellow leaves, tiny fake pumpkins, and all types of seasonal bullshit and hung it on my door. As soon as Thanksgiving passed, all my neighbors took down their fall wreaths and put up Christmas decorations instead. I went *back* to Walmart and bought a big-ass red-nosed reindeer, a giant blow-up snowman, and a plastic baby Jesus and put all that shit in the yard. On Halloween, Easter, Fourth of July—whatever my neighbors did to give their homes the holiday spirit, I tried to do even better.

I did everything I could to blend in. I went to every Little League game, school recital, and PTA meeting. I celebrated each passing season with the appropriate decorations. Still, I was always on edge, worried that one of them would clock that I hadn't grown up in this kind of middle-class, house-decorating lifestyle. I was especially paranoid about Donna.

One afternoon, about a year after we moved to Riverdale, Donna came knocking on my door. She was carrying a paper shopping bag filled with pairs of little girls' shoes, hand-me-downs from her daughter, Celeste.

"Hardly ever worn," she said, holding out the bag with the already-been-worn shoes. She said maybe I would have some use for them, seeing as I had "so many girls" of my own. She was trying to be slick. But I knew exactly what Donna was up to. This was her way of saying, "You *must* be struggling, with all them kids you got." Damn right we was struggling. But that was none of her damn business.

I was so mad that I left Donna standing on the porch and marched into the kitchen to grab a skillet. When Michael asked what I was doing, I told him, "I'm about to whoop that lady's ass."

"Now, Pat," he said in his Barry White you-need-to-calm-down voice. "You know out here, folks don't handle their business in the street."

Donna got lucky that afternoon. Michael took away my skillet and saved her from the ass whooping she had coming. But I felt so disrespected, I couldn't let it go. That Friday, I cashed my paycheck and went to Lenox Square mall out in Buckhead. The money was supposed to be for groceries. Instead, I spent a chunk of that change on a pair of full-priced Buster Brown girls' school shoes in size 4. I made sure the price tag was still attached when I dropped them off at Donna's door.

"Thank you so much for the used shoes," I told her, with a fake smile plastered on my face. "I have this extra pair of *brand-new* shoes. They're too big for my girls. You can have them. I know your daughter don't usually wear shoes as nice as this," I added. "I sure hope they fit." After that, me and Donna didn't talk much anymore.

That's how it was in Riverdale. I spent half my life looking over my shoulder, searching for signs of disrespect. The rest of the time, I was hard at work planting flowers and hanging wreaths and buying new shoes I couldn't afford for a neighbor I didn't like, just to act like I belonged.

For years, I didn't tell anybody in Riverdale—even folks I came to call good friends—that I was an ex-convict, or that my sister was hooked on drugs. I didn't let anybody know that I dropped out of school in eighth grade or that I got my job as a medical assistant through the Welfare-to-Work program. But the detail of my life I worked hardest to keep secret was that the only way me and Michael were able to afford living in their nice-ass neighborhood was because we were renting the house on Section 8. I thought if I kept up appearances, they'd never figure it out.

CHAPTER 4

PARQUET FLOOR

Before we moved to Riverdale, I never felt any shame about getting public assistance. That welfare-and-food-stamps lifestyle was all I'd ever known.

I came from generations of poverty. In my family, there was no money to pass down, no family business to take over. No one owned any property, and no one had any hope that things would ever get better. No one told me to get an education, because what was the fucking point? We was broke and we was always gonna be broke, was the mentality. Every day was only about survival. That meant doing illegal shit for quick money or trying to scam the government for more benefits to get by.

My granddaddy ran a bootleg liquor house out of his living room. My mama kept our lights on by "borrowing" electricity from her neighbors. My brother Andre robbed houses. My brother Dre stole bicycles that students parked on campus at Georgia Tech. My aunt Marvette had the craziest scam of all. She had five children. Whenever she met with her caseworker, she told her kids to "act retarded" because we all heard you got special benefits for kids with special needs. There was no shame in her game. That's the kind of ingenuity I grew up with. Those were the life skills I was taught.

I didn't fully understand all the different ways that middle-class folks looked down on people like me until we moved to Riverdale. My manager at McDonald's liked to play talk radio in his office. When I was in the back mopping the floors, I'd listen in to regular folks who called the radio station to share their complaints about the world. One of the most popular topics was "lowlifes" on public assistance. I heard "welfare queen," "fraud and abuse," and "the government is just handing out money to these people" more times than I could count. It was a real eye-opener to learn that middle-class folks thought the government was giving "free rides" to a bunch of lazy and worthless bums.

The fact is, Section 8 is for people who really need it, like old folks on fixed incomes, disabled people, and low-income families with little kids. The problem with Section 8 isn't that too many folks is on it. The problem is there's not enough supply to go around. These days in Georgia, folks have to enter a lottery for a chance to get on the Section 8 *waiting list*. Even if you win a spot, it might take several more years to actually get a voucher. A few years ago, almost two hundred thousand people applied for a waiting list lottery that only had fifteen thousand spots. The system is broken, but not because poor folks are getting a free ride.

In Riverdale, I didn't want my neighbors to think I was a lazy "welfare queen." I wanted them to see me as equal. At first, I just tried to hide that we were on Section 8. But when I realized they was all homeowners, I didn't even want them to know we were renting. I wanted what they had. So, I decided to fake it. In what would be my first acting gig, I started pretending that I *owned* that damn house. I acted the part so well, I almost convinced myself.

At the park, or the rec center, or while sitting on the bleachers at the kids' baseball field, I'd hear other parents talking about home renovations and work my way into their conversations.

"I'm thinking of cream tiles for the kitchen backsplash," Rhonda, a lady I recognized from up the block, was telling a group of mothers one afternoon at baseball practice. "Because the countertop is granite, *beige* granite, mind you, not gray, so it's all in the same color family. Warm and *earthy*."

"Tasteful," said a mother named Maryanne.

"And with the oak cabinetry," added Joan. "Very rustic."

I didn't know what the hell rustic cabinets were or why anybody would want an earthy kitchen. But I nodded and smiled and said I was thinking of remodeling my kitchen, too. "Me and my husband is updating our upstairs bathroom," I added. "I'm putting in a phone beside the toilet." To me, a toilet phone was the height of sophistication.

"Oh," said Rhonda, looking confused. "A phone in the *restroom*?"

"They come in different colors," I explained. "So you can match the phone to the shower curtain and toilet seat cover."

My Riverdale neighbors loved them some home improvements. One would be remodeling her kitchen and the other would be building a patio on the back of the house. To keep up with these folks, I realized I needed to do more than just *talk*. I had to show and prove. I got Michael to put in a new glass door and pressure wash the house. I planted an even bigger flower bed in the front yard. Then I discovered HGTV, which renovated my life.

On every HGTV show a host explained how to turn a raggedy or run-down piece of shit into something beautiful. No project was too big or too complicated or too ambitious. The hosts were always jolly, like putting in a new light fixture was the most fun they ever had. Pretty soon, I was watching HGTV the way Mildred watched her soaps. Anytime I had a free minute, I'd be glued to the set, mesmerized by all the home improvement projects. I loved the way the hosts made me feel like I could do anything I put my mind to.

One afternoon, I tuned in to watch a slim white lady with sparkly earrings telling me how easy it was to lay down a beautiful parquet floor. She was smiling her ass off, installing that flooring in full makeup and perfect hair. The finished floor looked impeccable and classy. I glanced down at the ugly green carpet in our living room, turned off the TV, and took my ass to Home Depot. I wanted a brand-new parquet floor, too.

When Michael came home that evening, he found me on my hands and knees, hard at work ripping up the green rug. "You sure Ms. Gertie's okay with this?" he asked. "Did you even ask her before you started?"

Michael was big on getting permission. But I thought it was stupid to ask about doing something when you already knew the other person was gonna love it.

"I can't remember," I lied.

Michael helped me take out the rest of the carpet. When we was done, I stared at the dingy plywood we'd uncovered. I had no idea what we were supposed to do next. I'm not no contractor; I don't have these skills. My dumbass hadn't even taken any notes while the HGTV lady explained her process. And I couldn't look up "how to do floor installation," because YouTube didn't exist yet. Instead, me and Michael had to freestyle, figuring it out for ourselves. "It's light work," I told Michael, trying to sound confident. "That white lady did it without messing up her makeup. This ain't nothing for us."

The flooring came in pieces that were supposed to fit together like a giant jigsaw puzzle. We spent all weekend measuring, hammering, and gluing that shit. But when we finished, our brand-new parquet floor didn't look anything like it did on TV. It was a hot-ass mess.

It turns out that before you lay down a floor, you need to make sure that the subfloor underneath is perfectly level. I must have missed that part of the show. The plywood in our living room was all kinds of warped and uneven. When we put down the new flooring, none of the pieces lined up. It was so janky you could stub all ten toes just from walking across the room.

As bad as it looked, Ms. Gertie loved it, just like I'd predicted. The way she carried on, thanking me to the heavens, you'd think we had built her the Taj Mahal. "Oh, Patricia," she gushed. "You're fixing this place up *so* nice." She thought I was the perfect tenant, renovating her run-down house for free. Really, my beautification projects were just part of my homeowner impersonation. Ms. Gertie was praising me for being a fraud.

CHAPTER 5

HOUSE RULES

The kids were at school, Michael was at work, and I was in bed for the day, enjoying some peace and quiet. I'd recently gotten myself unemployed from my McDonald's job after my manager asked me to do some stupid shit and I told her, "No, thank you. I'd rather not." Only, I said it with spicier words and a stank attitude.

At home, I settled into the morning TV lineup: *The Price Is Right*, followed by *The Young and the Restless*, *The Bold and the Beautiful*, and *Guiding Light*, the same shows my mama loved when I was little. Mildred watched soap operas to lose herself in other people's problems. But I watched to see how rich folks like Jill Abbott and Nikki Newman decorated their houses. During the commercial break between *The Young and the Restless* and *The Bold and the Beautiful*, I dipped into the kitchen to get myself a Jimmy Dean breakfast sandwich and a glass of water, because we didn't have anything good to drink.

On my way back to bed, I glanced out the living room window and got the biggest jump scare of my life. The Section 8 home inspector, Mr. James, was walking up my driveway.

Earlier that year, Clayton County Housing Authority had sent me a letter with the date for Mr. James's yearly inspection. I'd hung the notice on the fridge with a magnet so I wouldn't forget. But that was in August. The appointment was for October. By then, the letter was buried under a mess of school permission slips, Little League schedules, and photos of the kids.

I needed time to prepare for an inspection. When I saw Mr. James coming toward the house, I damn near had a coronary.

For folks like me, who like to do things their own way, the problem with government programs, like Section 8, is all the rules and regulations. I thought some of those rules were stupid. They didn't fit with my lifestyle. So I was always trying to find a work-around, a loophole, a way to ignore the regulations, without getting caught.

The most annoying Section 8 rule is that only "authorized" people "approved" for the voucher are allowed to live in the Section 8 rental. Let's say you're a single mama with six children. Then one day you meet a man, fall in love, and he wants to move in and help you raise those babies. According to Clayton County Housing Authority, his "unauthorized" ass is not allowed to stay with you in your Section 8 home. So now you gotta choose between your rent voucher and a father figure for your kids. This is the kind of nonsense you need to work around when you're poor.

Michael and I had been together more than a year when we moved to Riverdale. But I told my caseworkers—at the Division of Family & Children Services, the welfare office, and the Housing Authority—that I was raising those six kids by myself. That meant that when Mr. James came by for his yearly inspection, I had to make it look like Michael didn't exist. Some folks might say I was "cheating" the system. But to me, this was good money management and common sense.

When we first moved in, I had my minimum-wage job at

McDonald's and Michael was working at the Simmons mattress factory. On the weekends, he made some extra money doing construction. If we both worked eight hours a day, five days a week, for fifty weeks a year, plus whatever Michael made doing construction, we'd have a combined income, before taxes, of around forty-six thousand dollars. I was scared that amount might put us into the no-man's-land where you're poor as hell, but you still earn too much to be eligible for Section 8. So I didn't dare report to the authorities that I had a hardworking man living in the house. Telling the truth was too risky.

As a home inspector, Mr. James's job was to make sure Ms. Gertie was keeping the property to the appropriate "livable" standards required by Section 8. Once a year, he checked that the electric was on and the water was running, and that the fridge was cold enough to store food. He wasn't there to investigate the tenants. But I knew that if he saw signs that an unauthorized person was living in the house, he'd contact my caseworker and rat me out for sure.

I'm a big-boned, big-breasted woman. Normally, you won't see me running unless it's from the police. But that morning when I saw Mr. James, I took off like Jackie Joyner-Kersee.

I raced to our bedroom. Michael's stuff was everywhere. I grabbed jeans and T-shirts and half a dozen HBCU sweatshirts he liked to wear from the closet and shoved them under the bed. I took the Malcolm X, Atlanta Braves, and Cross Colours ball caps he had stacked neatly on the dresser, threw them in the shower stall, and pulled the curtain closed. I took his shoes, which Michael had carefully lined up under the bed, toes out, like he was still in the military, and put them in Nikia's bedroom, hoping Mr. James wouldn't wonder why my seven-year-old son wore size 13 Reebok Classics.

"You okay?" Mr. James asked when I finally opened the front door, all hot and sweaty.

I told him I was doing aerobics. He looked me up and down. I was dressed in an oversize nightshirt and no bra.

"That your exercising outfit?" he said with a smirk.

"Yes, sir," I answered. "This outfit is why they kicked me out of the gym."

Mr. James took a clipboard from his briefcase and started making his way around the house. I trailed after him from room to room as he looked in closets, opened bathroom cabinets, and stuck his head inside my fridge. He'd finished snooping and was about to leave when he glanced down and caught sight of Michael's Craftsman toolbox and the black paratrooper boots he wore doing construction sitting right there by the front door. In all the commotion that morning, I'd forgotten to hide the most incriminating evidence: work boots and a toolbox were a dead giveaway that I had a man and that my man had a job.

"Those are my brother's," I said quickly. "He left them here. He's in jail." At least that last part was true.

"That right?" asked Mr. James, eyeing the toolbox. He leaned down, opened the lid, and peered inside, like he was checking to see if it was in good condition. "Looks like you probably don't have much use for this," he said slowly. "With no man in the house and all."

I nodded yes, because what the hell else could I do?

Mr. James left our house that afternoon with Michael's toolbox. In exchange, he pretended he didn't notice the size 13 boots by the door.

Mr. James never did report me for having an unauthorized tenant living on the premises. For a while, I got away with breaking the rules. But a few years after we moved to Riverdale, I committed an even worse Section 8 violation: I got myself a good-paying job and tried to keep it a secret.

It was 7:50 a.m. and I'd just finished rushing around the kitchen heating up Tennessee Pride sausage biscuits from the freezer, wrapping them in paper towels, and handing them to the older kids as they ran out to catch the school bus.

"Bye, Ma!" Nikia yelled as he slammed the front door behind him. I was turning to go back upstairs to put on my scrubs for my medical assistant job when the phone rang with a call from my friend Luella. She worked at the General Motors plant out in Doraville and was calling to let me know that GM was hiring temporary workers. "If you want the job," she said, "I can put in a referral for you."

Employee referrals is how regular folks do nepotism. I got hired right away. A few months later, Michael's sister-in-law, Betty, who also worked at GM, gave him a referral and he started temping on the assembly line, too.

The Doraville plant made Chevrolet, Pontiac, and Oldsmobile minivans. My job was in the paint department. When a car body came down the line, I had to pump sealant around any cracks and crevices around the doorframes and wheel wells to prevent carbon monoxide from leaking inside the cabin. I had to do this while the car was still moving on the conveyor belt. I had less than forty-four seconds to complete the task. Then I'd have to walk—or sometimes run—back to my station to catch the next car as it came down the line. Michael called it "chasing cars." The work was boring as hell. And standing for eight hours on a hard concrete floor was hard on my body. But I was making almost twenty dollars an hour, which was twice what I got paid as a medical assistant. In fact, GM paid better than any legal job I'd had before.

As a temp, I was only allowed to work for a maximum of ninety days. Then I got "laid off." But I could go right back the next day or a week or two later and get hired for another temporary position. We didn't get benefits, but the money was so good I quit my job at the doctor's office so I could put in more hours at the plant.

With overtime, in one month I made almost five thousand dollars. I felt like I'd won the lotto. I went out and got us a maroon living room suite from Havertys, with a sofa and a matching love seat. "Don't none of y'all sit on my new furniture," I told the kids. "Y'all wanna sit somewhere? Sit on the damn floor."

A few weeks after GM laid me off from my first temp position, they rehired me for another three-month gig. After years of struggle, it felt like we were finally on the road to getting ahead.

I'd been working on and off at GM for the better part of a year when I got a letter from the Clayton County Housing Authority telling me I needed to come in for my Section 8 recertification. I knew I'd broken the rules by not telling them about my GM gig. But I wasn't worried at all.

Back then, it was common knowledge that the Housing Authority had some janky-ass computer system that didn't automatically update your employment information. Instead, the agency relied on tenants to self-report their income. If I didn't tell the Clayton County Housing Authority that I had a new job, nobody would ever know.

A few weeks later, I was sitting in a cramped office grinning at my caseworker, Ms. Buckman, getting ready to play in her face. Her desk was covered in neatly stacked piles of paper. A coffee mug that claimed she was the "World's Best Mom" was turned out to face me.

"Ms. Williams," she began, looking over the "Declaration of Household Income" form I'd filled out. "I see you reported income from your job as a medical assistant."

"Uh-huh."

"But you're no longer working there?"

"No. That job didn't work out."

"And have you had any other employment?"

"No, ma'am. I'm unemployed."

She raised her eyebrows, then looked hard at her computer screen. She clickity-clacked, then turned back to me. "It looks like you also worked at General Motors."

I felt my heart skip a beat. When I'd filled out my income form, I hadn't put anything about my temp work at GM. There was no way the Housing Authority lady could have known what I was up to. And yet, she started reading from her computer screen the dates I'd been hired at GM and the wages I'd been paid.

Without letting me know what they were up to, the Housing Authority had revamped their computer system. Thanks to Bill Gates and his damn software updates, the lady in charge of my Section 8 voucher knew all about my life.

"I *had* a job at GM," I tried to explain. "But it was *temporary*. So I don't work there no more."

The Housing Authority lady took off her glasses and rubbed her eyes like she was exhausted. "Ms. Williams," she said, "you are required to report any and all employment, including temporary and part-time positions."

"I didn't know that," I lied.

"So what we're looking at here is 'unreported income,' which is a serious violation," she continued. "You understand that this is fraud?"

"I don't know nothing about all that."

She stared back at me for a long time, like she was trying to decide if she believed me. I fixed my face to look innocent. It must have worked.

"We'll chalk this up to a misunderstanding," the Housing Authority lady said, her voice softening. "But moving forward, you need to report *all* income sources. You'll also need to reimburse the department for the rent we paid your landlord on your behalf while you were working at GM."

She took out a calculator, punched in some numbers, and told me I owed the state of Georgia three thousand eight hundred and forty-eight dollars. She said she would put me on a payment plan. "Fifty dollars a month, for the next seventy-seven months, and your arrears will be paid off in full." She smiled, like she was waiting on me to thank her.

"Seventy-seven months?"

"Yes, that's six years," she said, peering at me over the rim of her glasses. "I trust you won't let this happen again."

I was lucky. I'd been caught hiding my income and got off with a warning. But it would take more than a warning for me to change my ways. I was trying to protect the family's resources. So the next year at my annual Section 8 recertification, again I didn't report my full income to the government. The Housing Authority was done with my bullshit. When I got caught the second time, they removed me from the Section 8 program for good.

The crazy thing is, if I'd told the truth, my rent would have only gone up maybe by a few hundred dollars. And I would have been able to stay in the program and recertify for more Section 8, if times got tough. But I wasn't thinking about what made sense for the long term. I was acting on instinct and home training.

I was raised to believe that whenever you're dealing with a caseworker or government agency, you should automatically hide information. We didn't trust nobody, so we was always playing defense, trying to guard what little we had.

Rich folks do the same damn thing. They lie and scheme and cheat the system all the time. Only when they do it, they have teams of lawyers, accountants, and financial advisors to help them find loopholes, write-offs, and cover-ups. Poor folks don't have those support systems. When we do financial shenanigans, we have to figure shit out on our own. That's why we always getting caught.

A few weeks after the Housing Authority cut off my Section 8 voucher, I got a letter from the Division of Family & Children Services. They were cutting off my food stamps, too.

Me and Michael had a good few years in Riverdale, but now that was over. We were in struggle mode, doing our best to get by.

CHAPTER 6

AND BABY MAKES TEN

After I lost my Section 8, Michael and I were stretched to the limit. Our rent shot up to six hundred dollars a month. We also had to pay the car note, after-school activity fees, credit card bills, and for groceries to feed all those kids.

We weren't in the best financial position to have any more children. But growing up poor taught me that if you wait until you have enough money to do something, you'll never do anything at all. I wanted to give Michael a baby because I loved him. And he deserved it. He was already raising a bunch of kids, at least one of them babies should have his last name. That would cement our family bond. Plus, Michael wasn't the type to walk out on his own children. If we had a baby together, it meant he wouldn't leave. That's some hood logic, I know. It don't always make sense.

We'd been living together in Riverdale for three years and I still wasn't pregnant. So I went to the gynecologist for an expert opinion. The doctor asked me what type of briefs Michael wore.

"I don't know the name," I said. "They white."

"Are they snug fitting?" the doctor asked. "Because you don't want the testicles sitting too close to the body. Body heat can affect motility, meaning the sperm don't swim as fast." The doctor waved his hands in the air like little fans. "You need to let the boys *breathe*," he explained.

"What are these for?" Michael asked later that night when I handed him a package of doctor-approved old-man boxer shorts I'd bought at Walmart to replace his tighty-whities.

"You been roasting your balls on a spit," I said. "All your sperms got the heat stroke. We need to cool them off."

Michael wore those breezy boxers for almost a year and *still* didn't get me pregnant, so I went back to the doctor for a follow-up. That's how I found out Michael's hot nuts wasn't the problem. There was something wrong inside me.

When I was fifteen, I got pregnant by the same low-down dirty dog pedophile who'd already got me pregnant twice before. That deadbeat wasn't helping me take care of the two children we already had. I knew there was no way I could raise a third baby on my own.

I went to Grady Memorial Hospital, where I'd delivered my first two babies, to get an abortion. This was back when abortions were safe and legal and covered by Medicaid. It should have been a quick and simple procedure. But I was a poor Black girl who showed up for her appointment without a parent or guardian, or even a boyfriend. Instead of giving me top-notch care, I think the doctors took one look at me and decided I'd be a good patient to use for practice.

I remember two white ladies in white doctor's coats standing over me. The younger doctor kept glancing at the older one with a worried expression that told me she didn't know what the hell she was doing.

I started bleeding. Not a little, either. I could feel hot liquid gushing out between my legs. I heard the younger doctor tell the older one, "I can't make it stop."

Afterward, the older doctor told me I needed to stay in the hospital for a few days. "Just to make sure you're healing up okay," she said. She tried to act casual, as if hemorrhaging like a stuck pig was no big deal. But I knew plenty of girls who'd had abortions, and it was always an in-and-out procedure. If you went to the clinic at ten in the morning, you could be at the club that same night.

Those Grady doctors never explained what happened inside me. Nobody ever told me what the younger doctor had done wrong. But in Riverdale, when I told my gynecologist about the abortion I'd had as a teenager, he sent me to get a fluoroscopy to see what was going on.

At the radiology clinic, a technician had me lie on my back in a darkened room lit only by the glow from her monitor. She inserted a speculum into my vagina and injected a giant syringe of contrast dye inside me. On the screen, I could see the liquid travel up my tubes; then it stopped and rolled back down. "Hmm," the technician said.

"What's that mean?" I asked.

"I'm not a doctor," she replied. "You really need to speak with your provider."

She squirted more liquid inside me. This time I looked away.

"Scar tissue," the doctor explained when I went back for my follow-up appointment. He took out a pad of paper and drew me a diagram of the female reproductive system. "I suspect that the procedure you had in the past may have created scar tissue, which is now obstructing one of your fallopian tubes." He looked down at his diagram and drew a big *X* to show how one tube was all blocked up. "I'm so sorry," he said. "There's really nothing we can do."

Two months later, I was pregnant.

A nurse would later tell me that sometimes the pressure from the fluoroscopy can loosen up a blockage. I don't know if my doctor forgot to tell me that might happen. Probably he didn't even know. A couple of years after he told me that I couldn't get pregnant, my doctor lost his medical license. The last time I saw him, he was standing in line at the unemployment office trying to find a new job.

Michael said if we had a girl, he wanted to name her Jasmine, after Jasmine Guy, the skinny light-skinned actress from *A Different World*. I told him if the baby was a boy, we were naming him Malik, after actor Malik Yoba, who played a sexy detective on *New York Undercover*. It's a good thing me and Michael watched so much TV, or that baby wouldn't have a name.

During my first trimester, Michael got sick as a dog. He was tired and puking and having all kinds of cravings. Meanwhile, I felt fine. Until one Sunday afternoon at the beginning of my fourth month, when we went over to my niece's house.

Michael was outside playing with the kids. I was lounging on the sofa. When I stood up, I felt a gush coming from between my legs. "Pat," my niece said, sounding alarmed. "Girl, you *bleeding*."

At Grady Hospital, I was put in a bed set at a thirty-degree angle so my feet were higher than my head. "We're using gravity to help keep your little one inside you," the nurse said, giving my hand a squeeze.

The doctor looked serious. He told me that it was too soon to deliver. "We really need to get to at least twenty-five weeks' gestation for the baby's heart and lungs to develop," he added. I was only at week twenty-one.

I was willing to do whatever it took to save our baby. Even if it meant spending four weeks in that upside-down bed. It was damn uncomfortable. But the baby was worth it. She was going to make our family whole.

Michael wanted to stay with me at the hospital. But I told him I'd be fine—plus, the kids needed him at home. I lay in that uncomfortable seesaw hospital bed for hours with my blood rushing to my head.

It must have been sometime around 2 a.m. when I began to feel contractions. I pressed the call button for help. When nobody came, I started hollering: "The baby tryna get out!"

A nurse rushed in, lifted the sheets, and stuck her fingers inside me to see if I was dilating. Then she ran out to get the doctor. "I think my water just broke," I said when he arrived.

The contractions came on harder. A nurse held my hand. The doctor laid a hand on my stomach and said, "I'm going to need you to push."

Jasmine Malik Lee was born on June 24 at 3:37 in the morning. The nurse wrapped my tiny baby in a blanket and placed her on my chest. I kissed the top of her head and held her close. She weighed fourteen ounces and was eleven inches long. Her eyes were still fused together. She had her father's nose.

That little girl was a fighter, like her mama. She survived for almost an hour and a half. The nurse said, "I'm so sorry," as she took my dead baby away.

Michael was devastated. When he got to the hospital the next morning, he took one look at me and my empty belly, and his eyes filled with tears.

"I don't understand how this happened," he kept repeating. "You were *fine* yesterday. I felt the baby kicking! This don't make no sense at all."

Michael is the most calm and levelheaded person I've ever known. But after losing our baby, it was like he temporarily lost his own mind. In the hospital room, he started pacing back and forth, talking about how he needed to go see my gynecologist. I could tell that Michael didn't want to have no type of conversation. He was finna kick that doctor's ass.

I tried to make him feel better. "I don't know why you're so upset," I said. "We can do this again next month." I guess that wasn't the right thing to say, because he looked at me like I was the most coldhearted bitch in the world, then left to go call his mama.

Michael's mother was a God-fearing woman who was in church every Wednesday, Friday, and Sunday. On Saturdays, she went twice. She probably told her son that this was God's will and that the Lord is near to the brokenhearted. Whatever she said soothed him, because when Michael came back into the room, he was calm.

I'd never seen Michael cry before. I was surprised when I saw his tears. Where I come from, a miscarriage is just another shitty thing that happens sometimes. And when bad things happen, you don't get to stop and boo-hoo and get lost in your feelings. You pick yourself up and keep it moving. It wasn't until I started making friends with middle-class, college-educated folks that I discovered some people grieve a miscarriage like they lost a full-grown child. I guess the pain of a miscarriage hits harder when your life isn't already filled with disappointments and heartache. When I lost Jasmine, I pushed my sadness so far down I couldn't even feel it.

Just like I'd predicted, a few months later I was pregnant again. The doctor told me I had a weak cervix, which meant the baby would have a hard time staying inside. I didn't have this condition with my first two babies. This was another problem caused by the jacked-up abortion I had back in the day.

I know some folks might want to twist this story and use it to make a case against abortions. To be clear: I don't think anybody should tell a woman what to do with her body, her vagina, or her life. If I want to stick firecrackers up my pussy and blow that shit up, that's my choice. I had complications from a bad abortion. But that doesn't mean all abortions are wrong, and it sure don't mean they should be illegal.

To keep the new baby inside me, my doctor gave me a cerclage, stitching up my cervix to keep it closed. He also told me I needed to take it easy and try to stay off my feet. I couldn't quit my job at GM, because we needed the money. But when my ninety days was up, I didn't apply for a new gig on the assembly line. I took a job that I thought would be easier on my body. I started working as a Walmart cashier instead.

Walmart said they paid hourly workers more than minimum wage. Which sounded good until you factored in that Georgia's minimum wage back then was one of the lowest in the country. I worked a forty-hour week; my take-home pay was two hundred and eight dollars *before* taxes. The first time I saw my paycheck, I broke down and cried. Eventually, I had to get a second job stocking shelves at Target during the overnight shift just to make ends meet.

Our daughter Michaela was born on a Wednesday afternoon in March 1999. Michael loved being a daddy to a newborn. He'd pinch her cheeks and kiss her belly and laugh his ass off every time she giggled. Before bed, he'd slick her hair down with Johnson's baby lotion and one of those little baby brushes. Then he'd rock her in his arms until she fell asleep. Watching Michael with our baby gave me the same warm feeling I had watching TV daddies loving on their TV kids, back when I was a little girl. Before Michael, I'd never seen that type of tenderness in real life. All my mama showed me about parenting was how to do things wrong.

A year after Michaela was born, I got pregnant again. This time we had a boy. We named him Michael Jr., but everybody called him Junebug. With my sister's four girls, my two older kids, and the new babies, we were now a family of ten.

In Riverdale, our home was loud and full of laughter. But with no Section 8 and no food stamps, we were scrimping and scrambling every day.

When Michael wasn't temping at General Motors, he was working a second job, framing houses. After almost a year and a half of working two jobs, Michael finally got a permanent position at GM. He was making union wages, plus benefits. We thought things would be easier. But then, a month into his new job, his damn car broke down. Michael had bought the beat-up 1964 Oldsmobile Cutlass from my brother. That piece of shit didn't even have seat belts. When it died on us, it set off a chain reaction, where the solution to one problem created a new problem and everything just kept getting worse.

"It's only temporary," Michael said, trying to reassure me the afternoon his car gave out. He was throwing jeans, socks, and T-shirts into his green army duffel bag. I was holding Junebug on my hip. Michaela had wrapped herself around my leg.

For his new job, Michael had to get to the GM plant in Doraville, about a forty-five-minute drive from home. We didn't live near any public transit that could get him there. But his mama did. Her place was a mile and a half from the Oakland City train station, in southwest Atlanta. Michael figured if he got up at three thirty in the morning, he could walk to the station, get the Gold Line to Doraville, and be at the GM factory in time for his 6 a.m. shift. "This isn't a forever situation," he promised. "I just need to save up a few paychecks so I can get another car."

"A few paychecks" sounded like "forever" to me. Until Michael got his money together, he'd be out of the house five nights a week leaving me to take care of eight kids on my own.

"This don't work for me," I told him.

In that calm tone he used that always made me mad, Michael

said, "Pat, you know I can't lose this job." He kissed the babies goodbye and told the big kids "mind y'all mama." Then he walked out of the house and left me all alone.

Michael thought he'd really done something coming up with this plan. But I wasn't trying to be a single mother just because his mama lived near the train. The next morning, I set out to solve this problem myself.

I cashed my little Walmart paycheck at the corner store, took the last sixty-two dollars out of our bank account, borrowed a couple of hundred more from James, the husband of my old caseworker Ms. Campbell, now my good friend. Then I asked Ms. Campbell if she could give me a ride to the buy-here, pay-here car lot. The car dealership had a giant NO CREDIT? NO PROBLEM billboard. That sign was calling my name.

The salesman showed me a 1996 burgundy Bonneville with ninety thousand miles on it. "I can sell this to you for six hundred down and five hundred a month for a thirty-six-month term," the salesman said. "That's an *exceptional* offer. Truly exceptional," he repeated.

We went back and forth until I got him to come down in price. I got the car for five hundred down, with a two-hundred-and-fifty-dollar car note due every other week.

"We do our own financing in-house," the salesman explained as he handed me a contract to sign. "That means you'll need to make your car payments right here, at the front office, in *cash*. We don't take no personal checks." He raised his eyebrows. "You okay with that?"

I was already working two jobs. I'd work three, if I had to. Just as long as it got Michael back at home. "We're good," I told the salesman. He gave me the keys, and I drove that car right off the lot.

I was so proud of my quick thinking and problem-solving skills. Every time Michael got in that burgundy Bonneville to drive to work,

I felt like I'd done good by my family. What I didn't know is that buy here, pay here is a scam. I'd fallen right into the trap.

One morning, about six months after we got our new car, Michael came running into the house talking about, "We got robbed." The spot where he'd parked the Bonneville the night before was empty. I dialed 911 and yelled at the dispatcher, "Send the police! Some nigga stole our car!"

The dispatcher asked me a few questions for clarification. She sounded like she'd done this a million times before. "Ma'am, your car was parked outside your home last night and you woke up and it was gone, correct?"

"That's what I just told you."

She asked for the car's license plate number along with the vehicle's make, model, year, and color. I heard clicking on the line as the dispatcher checked her computer. "Ma'am," she said, "the vehicle was repossessed by the lender. That's a civil matter, not a problem for the police. I'm afraid we can't help you." The line went dead.

Every two weeks for more than half a year, I'd been bringing two hundred and fifty dollars in cash to the buy-here, pay-here dealership, just like I was supposed to. I'd made practically every damn payment on time. I'd only missed the last two, and those buy-here, pay-here summabitches just rolled up on our house and took my damn car, which I realized was their plan all along.

Here I was thinking that buy here, pay here was a great service, helping folks out of a jam. You didn't need good credit. You didn't need to go to a bank. They'd *still* sell you a car. But really, it was all a setup. They were just waiting for their customers to fail. If you had one bad month—and missed two or three payments—they'd snatch back the vehicle they'd already "sold" you so they could turn around and "sell" it to the next sucker. There was no grace period and no mercy. That place wasn't no dealership; it was a car-rental robbery scheme. The main victims were folks already struggling to get by.

There's a reason you won't find buy-here, pay-here car lots, rent-to-own furniture stores, payday lenders, or check-cashing stores in upscale neighborhoods. These companies make their money on the backs of poor folks.

I've seen a lot of scams in my lifetime. The folks who run these types of businesses are some of the dirtiest hustlers of all.

After our car got repo'd, me and Michael went to a regular dealership and found a used 1992 Mitsubishi Montero SUV with sixty thousand miles on it. This time, we financed through AmeriCredit. The company was supposed to be more legit than buy here, pay here, but to me it felt like just another hustle. Our interest rate was almost triple what they charged at a regular bank.

Between our car note, rent, food, clothes, diapers, school shoes, sports uniforms, and after-school activity fees, plus formal dresses for Ashley and LaDontay to wear to the ROTC ball, we were drowning.

You need nerves of steel to live in America when you're working-class poor, because when things go wrong, you have nothing to fall back on. No savings to tap into. No family to bail you out. You can't just "pick up the pieces" and "reinvent yourself"—those are middle-class luxuries. Me and Michael just had to figure shit out.

We did our best to hide our stress from the children, scrimping and saving, shopping sales, and cutting coupons. We was always doing poor-folk math in our heads: *If we pay the electric bill, will we have enough to cover groceries? If we* don't *pay the bill, how long before the lights get cut off?*

One day, I came home from work and found not a damn thing in the fridge for dinner and nothing in the freezer for breakfast the next day. I went to Kroger and filled my cart with spaghetti, tomato sauce, hamburger meat, and three boxes of Jimmy Dean frozen breakfast sandwiches.

The bill came to twenty-seven dollars and seventeen cents. I handed the cashier a check hoping the store manager wouldn't try to deposit it before the end of the week. There was only seven dollars and thirty-seven cents in our bank account. Payday was on Friday; I'd gone shopping on Wednesday afternoon. All I needed was a day and a half for that check to clear.

On the drive home, I sent up a prayer to God: "Dear Lord, please don't let them Kroger muthafuckas cash that check before Friday. This is Pat, your number one fan. Amen."

I guess I didn't make God's list of miracles to perform that day. Because the bank charged us thirty-five dollars in overdraft fees. We were fined another fifty dollars for "insufficient funds" by Kroger. The store manager got the police involved and I got a citation for "misdemeanor deposit account fraud." The fee for that minor crime was a hundred and twenty-five dollars. Being poor is too damn expensive.

You'd probably think that somebody like me, who grew up on food stamps and welfare, wouldn't have such a hard time being broke as an adult. But Mildred's poverty made sense to me: She never had money because she never had no damn job. But me and Michael weren't unemployed, lazy, disabled, alcoholic, *or* illiterate like my mama. We stayed grinding, holding down two, sometimes three or four different jobs. I thought life would be different for us. Instead, every day was a new problem, pushing us deeper in the hole.

For so long, I'd dreamed of stability, security, and a matching-curtains-in-the-windows lifestyle for my kids. But no matter how hard we worked, it felt like we weren't ever getting ahead. For the first time in my life, I began to understand the hopelessness that broke my mother's spirit. I had no idea how to turn this shit around.

We'd been living in Riverdale for almost five years when I climbed into bed one night and sent another prayer up to God. I'm not much of a churchgoer. But the two of us have a special relationship. I'll reach out to Him in desperate times. Like, "Dear Almighty Lord in heaven above, can you help me find my damn house keys, please." He don't always answer those type of prayers. But when I'm *really* in trouble, He comes through.

I didn't have a specific request that night. I just prayed for something—*anything*—that might put us back on track. "Please God, I know I asked you to help me out at Kroger, and you didn't. But this time, I truly need some help."

God has a sense of humor, that's for damn sure. He answered my prayer by sending me an angel. He poured all His grace and mercy into the body of my little old landlady who waddled like a duck.

CHAPTER 7

CON ARTIST

I almost bought a house once. It was back before I met Michael. I was sixteen years old and doing very well as an independent entrepreneur.

Selling drugs wasn't my dream job. I would have preferred to do something classy, like selling makeup at the mall. But in the mid-1980s, crack was a high-growth industry. There was so much demand, it was easy work. I didn't have to pitch or promote the product. I just had to stand on the corner and customers would find me. I sold my first dime bags at fifteen. In less than a year, I was making thousands of dollars a night. That's stupid money for a teenager. And I blew that money on stupid shit.

I bought my first car before I even had my license. An '83 Chevrolet hatchback. I got it just so I'd have a place to sit when I was working at night and the weather turned bad. As soon as I turned sixteen and got my license, I leveled up. I bought an '82 Cadillac Fleetwood with a burgundy ragtop for eight hundred dollars at auction. For five thousand more, I had my new ride custom-painted pearl white with gleaming flecks of gold. I spent another stack on big-ass twenty-two-inch Trues and Vogues tires with spoke rims and a Panasonic sound system. I dropped tens of thousands more on clothes, tennis shoes, and MCM purses, just for fun. When my niece CeCe wanted a flashy gold tooth, I took her to the dentist and paid for that, too.

It was my supplier, Lamont, who finally gave me a wake-up call. He told me there were other ways to spend my cash besides Red Lobster and shopping sprees. "You need to broaden your horizons," he said.

Even though Lamont dressed corny as hell—with his suede Hush Puppies, khaki Dockers, and round wire-rimmed glasses like Dwayne Wayne from *A Different World*—I had a little crush on him because he had his shit together. I was selling dope to support my kids. Lamont was dealing to pay off his college loans and save money for his future.

One afternoon while we were at my apartment doing business, Lamont nodded toward the stack of unopened sneaker boxes I had lined up against the wall. "Reckless spending," he said, shaking his head. "Consumerism is a trap."

"But they the new Jordans," I explained. "I got them in different colors."

Lamont let out a heavy sigh. "This is exactly what I'm talking about. If you keep spending on bullshit, you won't never get ahead." He told me to get my jacket and pack up the kids. "Take a ride with me," he said. "I want to show you a few things."

Lamont was always taking me on outings to show me fancy shit. When he didn't like the fake cherrywood dinette set I bought at Wolfman Gallery, he took me to Havertys to school me on what he called "quality home furnishings." When he saw me giving the kids McDonald's Happy Meals for dinner, he said, "With the money you making, y'all should be eating better than this," then took us to LongHorn Steakhouse. One time he brought me to Shane Company to show me diamond rings. "When you get married," he said, "make sure your man gets you something from a place like this. White gold," he added. "Keep it upscale."

The afternoon Lamont accused me of reckless spending, we drove for almost an hour, to a new housing development under construction, where we toured a model home. The bedrooms all had walk-in closets with custom shelving. The living room was carpeted in soft beige and the walls were painted creamy white. It was the kind of place where you step inside, and you automatically know you aren't supposed to cuss.

"Don't no niggas live like this," I whispered to Lamont.

He raised his eyebrows. "Who's *niggas*?" he shot back.

On the ride home, Lamont wouldn't stop talking. It was like being trapped in a car with a Black Tony Robbins. "You need to think bigger than buying a bunch of tennis shoes," he told me. "Invest in something substantial. Like property. Think about the future you want to give your kids."

I'd never before considered buying anything that didn't come from a car lot or the mall. But Lamont inspired the hell outta me. He was right. It was time for me to aim higher. Buying a house was next-level boss-bitch business, and classy as hell. No one in my family owned a place of their own. Now that I was making money, I could be the first.

I didn't know the first thing about real estate. How could I? They don't teach long-term investment strategies in middle school and I had to drop out in eighth grade to raise my kids. I knew I needed an expert's advice. But I was so young and dumb I turned to Duke—one of the worst fucking people in the world—and asked him to help me out.

Duke was the hood go-see man. As in, if you had a problem, go see Duke. You got a traffic ticket? He knew somebody at the courthouse who could fix it. Need a lawyer? He'd hook you up with some shady attorney to help you out. But his biggest operation was offering Mexican laborers help with getting their green cards. On Saturday mornings, they'd line up at Duke's front door waiting for their appointment. Duke charged a couple of hundred dollars for his assistance. But it was all a hoax. That man didn't know shit about a green card. He was just selling a dream.

On the weekends, Duke was a one-man Republican Party, ruining the lives of hardworking immigrants. During the week, he had a legal job in an office building downtown. I don't know what the hell type of employment he had. But he was the only nigga I knew who wore a tie and hard-soled shoes to work.

"You know anything about buying a house?" I asked him a few days after I'd visited the beige-carpeted model home. "I want to get a nice three-bedroom for me and my kids."

Duke smiled with all his teeth: "Lemme see what I can do."

A week later, I was working my corner when Duke rolled up in his Buick Electra 225. "Girl," he said with his big-ass grin, "I done found you the perfect place." He leaned over to open the passenger-side door. "Let's go check it out."

We drove about ten miles out from Ashby Grove, turned onto a tree-lined street, and pulled up to a two-story redbrick house with a patch of burned-out grass out front.

"Not that one," Duke said. "Your house is the one over there."

It was so beautiful it took my breath away. The house, a low-slung L-shaped ranch, had pale yellow siding, dark brown shutters, and a tidy front yard. Duke pulled out a folded *Atlanta Journal-Constitution* from the glove compartment. "See here," he said, pointing to a "House for Sale" ad he'd circled in the middle of the page: "Charming three-bedroom, two baths, appliances like new. For sale by owner."

"What'd I tell you?" Duke asked. "Perfect for you and the kids."

The house looked good from the street, I agreed. But when I

asked Duke if I could go inside, he said maybe some other time. "The owners are funny like that," he explained. "But don't even worry about it. I already checked it out myself." He flashed me his toothy grin. "You know I gotchu, girl." According to Duke's home inspection, the interior was "upscale and luxurious."

"You ever heard of a BarcaLounger?" he asked. "The living room fits two or three of those type recliners, easy. As hard as you work, you *deserve* a nice place like this."

Duke's expression grew serious. "There's just one problem," he said. "Someone in your line of work can't just walk into a bank and get a mortgage. You gotta stay out of the spotlight. That type of financial transaction brings too much heat." Again, he told me I didn't need to worry because he was gonna help me out. Duke promised to deal with the bank and "handle all the paperwork" to make sure the deal was "copacetic" and "legit." All he needed from me to make it happen was ten thousand dollars in cash. "I only got five on me," I said, reaching into my pocketbook. "I can give you the rest tomorrow."

I gave Duke the money he needed, and he strung me along for a few weeks. Then one afternoon, he came by my block talking about how "the seller changed his mind," and my dream house was off the market. But when I asked for my money back, Duke said, due to "IRS auditing and whatnot," it wasn't safe to give it back all at once. He'd slide me a couple hundred here and there. In the end, he kept most of it for himself.

Getting played like that was a game changer. The experience taught me that telling other people my hopes and dreams made me an easy target. From then on, whenever I really wanted something, I made sure to keep it to myself.

In Riverdale, I still dreamed about owning a house for my children just like I had when I was a teenager. But this time, I didn't tell a soul. Not even Michael. Instead, I spent my days pretending I was a homeowner, putting up seasonal door wreaths and redoing the living room floor. Then at night, I let my imagination run wild, thinking up all the things I'd do if that house was really ours. I dreamed of a kitchen with custom-made cabinets and a bathroom with a telephone by the toilet.

Only me and God knew about my private fantasies. So when out of the blue I got an opportunity to make my dream come true, it felt like it was heaven-sent.

I was in the yard watering my petunias one afternoon when I looked up and saw Ms. Gertie waddling up the driveway. We chitchatted for a while about the weather and my flowers. She asked me about the kids. Then her tone got serious. She told me she was retiring from being a landlord and that she'd decided to sell the house.

"You and your family have been such good tenants," she added. "I'd really love for you to stay here. I don't want to put you out."

"I don't want you to put us out either," I said. I loved our lives in Riverdale. Even though we didn't own it, the house felt like our family's home. I hated the idea of starting over. It gave me flashback feelings from all the times I had to suddenly pack up my shit and move when I was young.

Ms. Gertie must have seen the worry on my face. She patted my arm and said, "Patricia, I've given this a lot of thought. If you're interested, I'd like to sell the house to you."

I stared back at her in disbelief. The last time I checked, I had seventy-eight dollars in my checking account. "I don't think I have enough money for a house," I told her. "I could maybe buy a window."

Ms. Gertie laughed and told me not to worry. She had the whole thing figured out.

She explained that she was going to sell me the house through something called "owner financing," which meant that instead of paying the mortgage to a bank, I'd pay it directly to her. She even offered to help me out with the down payment. "I've been putting away a little something from the rent every month ever since you moved in," she explained. She had five thousand dollars saved that she was going to give me to help me buy her house.

It sounded too good to be true. But I trusted Ms. Gertie. She'd never been anything but good to me. And I really wanted that house.

On a sunny day in June of 2002, I put on my nicest outfit—a pair of black slacks from Lane Bryant, a light-blue Ashley Stewart blouse—then drove to meet Ms. Gertie at her attorney's office.

It took almost an hour and a half for me to sign all the different documents her lawyer had prepared: a promissory note, a security deed, a purchase agreement. I didn't read not one damn page of any of those forms. I was so excited, I just wanted to get the deal done.

When we were finally finished, Ms. Gertie hugged me. "I'm so glad you're staying," she said. Her attorney smiled and shook my hand. I walked out of that office so high it felt like I was floating. I got into my car and drove directly to my favorite store, Home Depot, grinning ear to ear. I picked up a sledgehammer, a pair of work gloves, and some safety goggles. Now that I owned the place, I could finally start making good on all the HGTV home renovation projects I'd been dreaming about for years.

At home, I pulled into my driveway, flung open the front door, and headed straight for the kitchen. I started swinging my sledgehammer at the ugly kitchen cabinets I'd been hating since the day we moved in. This was *my house*. You couldn't tell me shit.

Years earlier, the trucker with the spider bite had tried to convince me that home ownership is a trap. But I didn't feel trapped. I felt so damn proud. No matter how bad things were out in the world, my children would always have a place to call home. With every swing of my sledgehammer, I was tearing down a generation of curses to create something beautiful in its place.

I don't know how long Michael was standing in the kitchen doorway watching me. I glanced up and there he was, his eyes as wide as saucers as he looked around at the mess. "Golly," he said, taking it all in. "It looks like a tornado ran through here."

I ignored him and pointed to the walls where the cabinets used to be. "I took them all down," I said. I thought Michael would be impressed. Instead, he just looked confused.

"But why didn't you just use a screwdriver?" he asked. "Taking down cabinets isn't really a sledgehammer-type job."

As much HGTV as I'd watched, I must have missed the show about easy kitchen cabinet removal. But I didn't care if it took more work. Swinging that sledgehammer was like I was doing a victory dance. A screwdriver wouldn't have been any fun.

For two years, I worked my ass off, trying to get my house the way I wanted. To save money, Michael and I did a lot of the renovations ourselves. But it was slow going. I still didn't have my toilet phone. And then, one afternoon, Ms. Gertie came by to visit again. This time she had a warning.

"I'm getting on up there in years," she began. We were sitting at the dining table on my freshly reupholstered chairs. I'd bought three yards of dark-brown imitation leather I'd found on discount and reupholstered the chairs myself. I got the idea from a lady on HGTV. "When I pass, the mortgage for this house will go to my children.

But they don't know you like I do . . ." Ms. Gertie added, her voice trailing off.

I'd known Ms. Gertie for seven years, and this was the first time I was hearing about her having any kids. I've never met a mother who doesn't talk about her babies. I figured Ms. Gertie's must be real bad if all this time she'd been acting like they didn't even exist.

"I'm worried about the situation," Ms. Gertie continued, confirming my suspicions. "For your protection, I think it would be better if you had a mortgage with a bank instead of continuing your mortgage with me." I didn't have the credit or finances to get a mortgage. Ms. Gertie told me not to worry. She had a plan to work it all out.

Her idea was for me to sell the house to Michael. With his full-time job at GM, she said, he'd have no problem getting approved for a mortgage. With the money I got from selling the house to Michael, I could pay off my debt to her. This was a lot for someone like me with limited financial literacy. Most everything I knew about money came from forging checks and selling crack. But Ms. Gertie made it all sound so simple. It turned out she was right.

On July 12, 2005, I sold the Riverdale house to Michael for $92,800. Seventy-eight thousand eight hundred dollars went directly to Ms. Gertie. The rest of the money, fourteen thousand, we took out in cash. I used it to finish my home renovations. I got all-new kitchen appliances and updated the bathroom with that wall-mounted toilet phone.

Michael and I didn't really understand the small print of the mortgage. But looking back, I think we got a pretty decent deal: a thirty-year fixed-rate mortgage at 6.5 percent. Our monthly payments were five hundred and seventy-seven dollars, which was lower than what we'd been paying in rent. We could manage. We were good. I'd gotten everything I'd wanted—we were now middle-class home-owning folks—but now I wanted more.

The American dream is all about aspiration, wanting and striving for better than you already have. But for me, the hunger also comes from growing up poor. It's like I have a little devil whispering in my ear, *What you have ain't enough.* That demon is how we ended up getting into all kinds of money trouble in Riverdale. And when I say "we," I mean "me." Michael never would have made all those bad decisions on his own.

Michael's sensible, thoughtful, and likes to take his time. When he makes a decision, he's the type to think it over, make a plan, then think about the plan some more. Like, if I said, "We need to paint these kitchen cabinets," he'd stand in front of the cabinets with a notepad trying to decide if we should paint the top or bottom first. Meanwhile, I'll have gone to Home Depot, picked up a gallon of paint, come back home, slapped on a coat, made myself a sandwich, and he'd *still* be standing there, staring at the cabinets like he was waiting on Jesus to fax him the answer.

For a long time, I thought we just had different personalities—Michael is molasses, slow and unbothered; I'm Flo-Jo racing to the finish line so I can get that gold. But now, I think we're different because of how we were raised.

Michael grew up with a stay-at-home-church-lady mama and a daddy with a good-paying union job. He had a hot breakfast every morning. At night, he slept in a clean bed with a pillow. That kind of easy living gave him the security to take his damn time. He never worried, like I did, that if he took too long making a decision that whatever he was thinking about would be gone.

In my house, I couldn't count on anybody for anything. When it came to basic life necessities—food, clothes, a place to sleep at night—I learned to grab what I could and run. As a child, moving fast was a matter of survival. It turned me into the most impatient adult you'd ever want to meet. I want more *and* I want it now. It looks like greed. Really, it's leftover childhood trauma. If I don't get it, I get scared it's gonna be gone.

Mixing big dreams with survival instincts and childhood trauma is how we got all the way fucked. And by "we" again, I mean "me." I dragged Michael right into the mess.

None of it would have happened without Vernetta. She's the one who gave me the idea. Vernetta worked at GM with Michael. She was a walking billboard for spending above your means. That chick had every luxury item of the early 2000s: a fully loaded Cadillac Escalade with TV screens in the back of each headrest, Louis Vuitton and Gucci designer purses, and iPods for all her kids. She also had a brand-new mini-mansion laced with all kinds of chandeliers. GM paid good wages, but not *that* good.

When I asked Vernetta how she paid for that big-ass house, she told me she got herself something called a low-monthly-payment, interest-only balloon loan. I didn't know what any of those words meant. She made it sound like the details weren't important. The deal was too good to pass up.

"Baby," she said, "you don't need no credit check or nothing. It's like the banks be *givin'* that money away."

All that talk of easy money got me thinking, *With all these kids, we really could use a bigger house.* In Riverdale, we had three bedrooms among the ten of us. The kids were sleeping on bunk beds; I had four girls in one room. After my talk with Vernetta, I started driving all over Atlanta looking for a house for sale. I found a perfect four-bedroom still under construction, in a quiet subdivision near Camp Creek. It had a bedroom suite on the first floor, which was good for me and

Michael because the two of us hate taking the stairs. If we got one of them loans Vernetta was raving about, we could afford the down payment. That's all I needed to know.

Vernetta's broker worked for a company called Decision One Mortgage. His office was on the fifth floor of an office building out in Alpharetta, about forty-five minutes away. The broker had messed-up teeth, sweaty hands, and a shiny gold watch. *Yellow* gold, I noticed, not the "upscale" white gold Lamont had said a person with good taste would go for. That unclassy broker got me talking all about the new house I wanted to buy, smiling and gassing me up. He said he could help me get my dream house, "no problem." All we had to do was use our Riverdale house as collateral and take out an interest-only home-equity loan.

"Once you buy the new place," he continued, "you can sell your house in Riverdale for a substantial profit." He talked like gold coins would be shooting out our asses as soon as we took out a loan with him.

He wrote a figure on a piece of paper and slid it across the table: *226*.

"That would be your low monthly payment," he said, tapping his pen on the page. "No money down, no income verification, and very reasonable terms. This loan is perfect for hardworking folks like you." Me and Michael signed the papers and walked out of that office with a loan that sounded too good to be true . . . and it was.

Just like millions of other folks, we'd been talked into getting a "subprime" home loan. These deals were so bad that by 2008, they'd send the whole damn country into a recession. That's the mess we got caught up in, all because I wanted more, more, more.

That Decision One broker was a smooth operator. He kept smiling in our faces, telling us how lucky we were. But not once did he mention the terms of our agreement: after fifteen years of paying two hundred and twenty-six dollars a month, the *entire* amount we'd borrowed—all *twenty-seven thousand, eight hundred dollars*—would be due in full, at once. And if we couldn't pay that whole amount when the loan came due, the bank could foreclose on our house.

After all that, we never did end up buying that new house in the Camp Creek subdivision. All we got from that deal was some cash in hand that seemed to evaporate as soon as we got it and a loan that we'd be paying interest on for the next fifteen years.

God doesn't like ugly. And he sure as hell did not like the ugly of Decision One Mortgage, the company that sold us that loan. Not long after we met with that shady broker, Decision One started getting sued by everybody and they damn mama. They were called out for targeting Black and Latino borrowers, deceiving them about the true costs of the loans and charging them higher fees and interest rates than white customers with the same financials. Decision One was accused of predatory lending, fakery, bullshitting, con artistry, and deception. The company settled a class-action discrimination lawsuit for six and a half million dollars. Black and Latino borrowers were only eligible to receive two hundred dollars each from the settlement. The lawyers were paid $1.8 million.

The main victims of the subprime mortgage swindle were low-income folks trying to chase the American dream. Millions of people, including Michael's friend Vernetta, lost everything when the banks foreclosed on their homes.

I try to see the good in people, but sometimes it feels like every damn body's got a hustle: Mr. James scammed himself a toolbox. Duke tried to sell me a house that wasn't his to sell. The Decision One broker smiled in my face because that dirty muthafucka got a commission every time he conned a new sucker into a bullshit loan.

Sometimes I even wonder about Ms. Gertie. I was so sure she was an angel sent from heaven just to help me out. But when I look back on what happened to the neighborhood after Ms. Gertie sold us the property, I can't help thinking that maybe that little old lady was working a hustle, too.

When Michael and I moved to Riverdale in 1993, the neighborhood was mostly white. But right around that time, the City of Atlanta was getting ready to host the 1996 Olympic Games. To revamp, they tore down a bunch of public housing projects, kicking thirty thousand low-income folks out of their apartments. The Housing Authority gave everybody Section 8 vouchers and told them to find someplace else to live. That's when Black folks started moving out of the city and into places like Riverdale. Once that happened, all my white neighbors packed up and moved away. By the time Ms. Gertie sold me the house, we only had one white neighbor left. "It's that great white flight," Michael said.

I didn't know that white people running away from their new Black neighbors had an official name. I also didn't know that when a neighborhood goes from mostly white to mainly Black, the real estate prices fall through the floor. Ms. Gertie acted like she was looking out for me. But maybe she was looking out for her finances. Was she an angel or a shark? Probably a little of both.

We still own that house in Riverdale. In 2025, me and Michael renovated the property so we could rent it to new tenants. We installed a new kitchen, an electric fireplace, a soaking tub, and a glass-enclosed shower with a rainfall showerhead. I posted all the renovations on TikTok.

I'll always love that house. It's a reminder of how far we've come. Like the story of my life, it's part beautiful and part ugly. I planted pretty flowers in the front yard and killed roaches in the kitchen. I achieved my goal of homeownership, but we also got conned into paying the bank tens of thousands of dollars that we didn't have to spare. I chased the American dream, but I was also lied to, tricked, and maybe even a little brainwashed along the way.

The trucker with the brown recluse spider bite had tried to warn me. But I guess I had to learn those lessons for myself.

CHAPTER 8

BAD CREDIT

I'll never forget the day I learned that Michael really loved me. We were standing at a cash register in a Sears department store, buying a pair of school shoes for my son. The checkout lady rang up the total, then turned to Michael. "May I interest you in an exciting in-store promotion?" she asked. She sounded like a robot. It was the same tone I used when I worked at McDonald's and asked customers if they wanted to supersize their meal. "If you open a Sears card," she continued, "you'll get ten percent off today's entire purchase. It only takes a few minutes to apply. You can do it right here in the store."

Michael shrugged. But I didn't want him to miss out on a good deal. I turned to the cashier and told her, "Hell yeah, he'll take it." She handed Michael a folded pamphlet. On the cover it said, in big bold letters: "Apply Today for a Sears Mastercard. Use It Everywhere Mastercard Is Accepted." Inside the pamphlet was a form to fill out. Michael wrote his name, address, birth date, name of employer, employer's address, and Social Security number.

When he was done, he gave the form back to the cashier so she could enter the information into the little computer beside the register. As she was typing, she looked up, glanced in my direction, then asked Michael if he'd like to include his wife as an authorized user. We'd only been living together in Riverdale for a couple of months. So I was shocked as hell when I heard Michael give the Sears lady my name. I was so damn excited. It felt like he'd dropped to one knee and was handing me a diamond ring. Making me an authorized user meant this love was for real.

Nobody in my family had a credit card. The only currencies we used was cash, food stamps, and the little stubs of paper that the numbers man gave Mama whenever she placed a bet. We also didn't trust banks. My granddaddy kept his money in an old sweat sock tied to his belt loop and tucked inside his pants. Before he got busted for selling drugs, my baby daddy kept his cash in a fanny pack like a gotdamn kangaroo.

Michael had more class. When we met, he already had a bank account, excellent credit, and US savings bonds he bought when he was in the military. He even had three different credit cards. None of them was a preloaded Baby Phat bullshit card, either. He had a Visa, a Macy's card, *and* a card for Circuit City. The first time I saw him take out his wallet and pay for gas using plastic instead of cash, I felt like I was dating a Black Victor Newman. I thought Michael was sophisticated and out of my league. That afternoon at Sears, it felt like he was pulling me into *his* world. I knew then that we was ride or die till the end.

Michael had no idea what he was getting into. If he had, I'm sure he would have told the Sears lady, "Hell no," and bought me a big-ass diamond ring instead.

A few weeks later, a Sears Mastercard with my name on it arrived in the mail. I immediately took my ass shopping to buy a few things for the kids. It felt so good to walk through the aisles, putting underwear, socks, T-shirts, and jeans in my basket, then hand my card over to the cashier. It's not like I'd never used a credit card before. Back in my criminal days, I went shopping with stolen credit cards and a fake ID all the damn time. But having a card with my real government name that matched my not-fake picture ID made me feel like I could hold my head up high. I enjoyed the hell outta legal credit card transactions.

A month later, the Sears bill came in the mail. I was surprised to see that we only owed thirty-five dollars, because I definitely spent more than that in the store. But there it was in black and white, "Minimum Payment Due: $35." *No wonder folks love credit cards,* I thought. *It really do take all the stress out of shopping!*

I had such a good time using my credit card, I started going shopping just for fun. I bought bedding and towels and a matching set to redecorate the bathroom. I got a mint-green toilet lid cover, a roll of mint-green bathroom carpeting that I could cut around the toilet for a wall-to-wall effect, and white curtains with mint-green trim for the window. The next week, I got us a toaster oven, a set of pots and pans, and a brand-new Kenmore vacuum cleaner to replace the perfectly good broom we had at home. I even splurged on a Sony camcorder so I could film the girls' cheerleading practice and make videos of Nikia playing sports. The great thing about that Sears card is that I could use it anywhere Mastercard was accepted. So I was whipping it out all over the place. I paid for gas, groceries, and tennis shoes at Foot Locker. When I saw a brand-new set of dishes at JCPenney, I used my Sears card to pay for those, too.

When the Sears bill came through the following month, Michael opened the envelope and stared at the bill in shock.

"How the hell did you max out the card?" he asked.

"What's that mean?" I replied.

That's how Michael discovered that his authorized user didn't know a damn thing about using a credit card. He sat me down at the kitchen table and explained that the "minimum payment due" is different from the "account balance," a way higher amount, which he said we should be paying in full. Then it was *my* turn to be surprised. All this time, I thought spending without paying was the whole damn point. Thanks to all my shopping, we owed thirty-five hundred dollars on that card.

After that, Michael tried to convince me that credit cards were for "emergencies only." To make his point, he brought up the "emergency" that happened a few months after we met.

I'd been pulled over for a traffic violation. When the officer ran my information, he found out I was driving on a suspended license. He slapped a set of handcuffs on me, put me in the back of his patrol car, and took my ass to Fulton County Jail. I got fingerprinted and mug shots taken and charged with a misdemeanor. Michael took a cash advance on his Visa card and paid the hundred-and-fifty-dollar bond.

My court date was set for two months later. But I didn't want to go. "I don't have time for all that bullshit," I told Michael.

"What's gonna happen next time you get pulled over?" he asked. "It's better to get this straightened out now." He promised to come with me to my court date. Once we got in front of the judge, I'm sure Michael wished he'd stayed home.

The judge looked down at me over his wire-rimmed glasses. "Ms. Williams," he said in a voice so deep it sounded like God himself was talking. "Are you aware that in addition to your charge of driving on a suspended license, you also have multiple outstanding citations?"

"No, sir," I said. "That must be some type of mistake."

He shook his head and began reading a list of my infractions: driving over the speed limit, failure to obey traffic signals, parking in a handicap zone without a permit, and improper parking.

"I'm a good driver," I interrupted. "I don't park 'improper.'"

"It means you were ticketed for parking in an improper zone," he explained. He looked at my file, flipping through the pages. "I see here a violation for parking in front of a fire hydrant. That's what we mean by 'improper.'"

"Thank you for the explanation, Your Honor," I said. "I guess maybe I did park—"

"In fact," he continued, cutting me off with a wave of his hand, "you seem to have committed this same violation on multiple occasions." He put down the manila folder filled with all my traffic sins and gave me a stern look. "Ms. Williams, I trust you are aware that you are *not allowed* to park willy-nilly wherever you so please. We have traffic laws in Georgia for a reason."

"Yes, sir. But that hydrant don't even work. Because when the house on the corner caught on fire—"

He cut me off again. "And yet, even after receiving *multiple* summons, you failed to appear in court."

"Yes, sir, but I don't remember—"

For a third time he cut me off. Michael had told me to go to court to straighten things out. But I didn't know how I was supposed to do that if this Barry White muthafucking judge wasn't interested in hearing anything I had to say.

The judge closed the folder and didn't even look up when he announced that the total amount I owed for "fines, surcharges, and multiple fees for failure to appear in court" was twenty-eight hundred dollars. He said I needed to pay a thousand that day or he'd send my ass to jail. "Ms. Williams, do you have the funds to settle these citations?" he asked.

That's when Michael came to my rescue. While I was in the holding pen, he ran to the ATM to get a cash advance on his credit cards to pay my fine. He could only take out five hundred dollars at once. I had to spend a night in jail. But that was still better than the month and a half the judge wanted me to serve for all those unpaid fines.

After he learned I'd maxed out the Sears card, Michael told me I needed to stop buying stuff we didn't need. "The main reason for these cards," he said again, "is for *emergencies*. We got all these kids. Anything could happen. You need to slow your roll."

I really did try to follow the program. It wasn't my fault that the first emergency that came up was the Fourth of July, a holiday that Michael didn't even understand.

Where I come from, the whole damn point of Fourth of July is to dress your kids in matching outfits of red, white, and blue with brand-new crisp white tennis shoes. We weren't celebrating the country. The holiday was an excuse to show out.

In Riverdale, I wasn't about to let my neighbors see my six kids looking raggedy on Independence Day. On July 2, I took Nikia to the barber for a haircut and brought the girls to the salon to get their hair permed and styled. The Sears card was maxed out. But Michael had a perfectly good Macy's card that he hardly ever used. On July 3, I slid that card out of his wallet while he was asleep and took my ass straight to the store. I bought six matching outfits and six new pairs of tennis shoes. The kids looked so sharp, like they stepped right out the pages of *Jet* magazine.

"I better not see not one of you running around or playing in no grass," I warned them before we left the house. "Get them clothes dirty and I'll beat all y'all asses."

Michael tried to tell me that most people don't treat the Fourth like the Ebony Fashion Fair. But I didn't believe him. At the Greenbriar Mall in Southwest Atlanta, where all the Black folks shopped, Foot Locker and Champs had lines out the door on July 3, with everybody buying new outfits for the cookout. For years, Michael tried to convince me that this wasn't regular behavior. Finally, I decided to investigate for myself. I took my ass to North Point Mall, in Alpharetta, the day before Independence. I was shocked to find no lines, no commotions, no big deal. It was just a regular day, business as usual. I came home and told Michael, "Dressing up for the Fourth of July is some nigga shit!"

"That's what I been trying to tell you," he said.

I didn't know this when we first moved to Riverdale. Back then, I went all out dressing my kids in brand-new patriotic outfits for the holiday. I did the same thing on Easter Sunday, Valentine's Day, and the first day of school. This wasn't only about special occasions. Making sure my kids were always clean and put together was one of the most important things I did as a mother.

When the July Macy's bill came, Michael, who never gets mad, hit the muthafuckin' roof. "You spent *four hundred dollars* on clothes?"

"And matching shoes," I clarified. "In fact, I *saved* you money. Nikia's tennis shoes was on sale."

"We out here struggling to cover the basics," he said. "And you out here buying stuff they don't even need. They got plenty clothes. There was no reason the kids need to look like a bunch of walking American flags."

That was our first big fight about money. And like most fights about money, it was really about something else. Michael felt like I didn't understand how much work he put into being financially responsible, and I felt like he didn't understand why I cared so much about the kids dressing sharp.

For me, this went way deeper than matching outfits. I was trying to protect my children and keep them safe the way nobody had looked out for me. This was an act of love.

When I was little, Mildred let me go out in the world looking any kind of way. I'd show up at school raggedy and musty, teeth unbrushed, hair not combed, dressed in secondhand clothes from the trash bags of donations my brothers stole from the drop-off bin outside the Goodwill. When a child is ungroomed and unkempt, it sends a message that nobody cares about them at home. At school, that made me a target. I got bullied all day, every day. I wasn't going to let that happen to my own kids.

Maybe Michael would have understood if I'd told him more about my childhood. He knew we were poor, that I went to school hungry, and that Mildred would beat me for no reason. But I never told Michael the story about Janice and her socks. To this day, he still doesn't know.

I don't know why Janice came to stay with us. Back then, my mama was the type to strike up a sidewalk conversation with a stranger in the morning. By the afternoon, that person would be living in our house. When I was in fifth grade, Janice suddenly appeared.

Janice was disabled. Or maybe she just had real bad posture. All I know is that lady had the worst case of knock-knees I ever saw. But it was her ankles that caught my attention. On the bottom of her bent-up legs, she wore the most beautiful pair of socks. They was brown with white ruffles and looked like something that Nikki Newman from *The Young and the Restless* would have worn when she was a little girl. Janice said proudly that she'd bought those fancy-ass socks with her Social Security check. She wore them day after day, until they were so hard and crusty they could stand up on their own. Those socks stank like a bucket of dead fish left out in the high noon sun. That stench could knock a grown man to the ground. I didn't care how they smelled. I thought those socks were glamorous.

The only nice thing Mildred ever bought me was a pair of

knockoff Sebagos from Payless. By the time I was in fifth grade, those shoes were two sizes too small. I had to wear them like a pair of slides, with my heels hanging out the back just to give my toes some room.

I didn't have shoes that fit or a single cute outfit. But I thought if I could rock those socks with the pretty ruffles, even for just one day, those evil-ass kids at school would leave me the hell alone. One night after Janice fell asleep, I tiptoed into the room and stole those socks right off the floor.

The next morning, I strutted into my fifth-grade classroom with my little sock ruffles on full display. I sat down at my desk and got comfortable, sliding my feet out the back of my too-tight shoes. I thought I was going to have a good day for once. Then I felt a tug on the back of my hair.

It was Roland, the short-ass bucktooth boy with the senior-citizen-looking face, who sat in the desk behind me. Roland was the class clown.

"Buckwheat," he said, making fun of my dried-out Jheri curl, his favorite topic. "Nappy-headed ho." He talked quiet enough so the teacher at the front of the class couldn't hear but loud enough to make all the kids around us crack up. "You helpin' yo' mama clean the oven," he continued, "with that Brillo pad on yo' head?"

I could feel my face burning up as the laughter swelled all around me. Then that dumbass tried to pull my hair again.

I stood up and turned toward him. With my desk stuck around my waist like a Hula-Hoop, I started smacking the shit out of Roland. I wanted to knock that smirk right off his old-man face. In all the commotion, my right shoe flew up in the air; my left shoe slid sideways across the floor. That's when the whole room filled with the aroma of Janice's funk-nasty socks.

"*Ooooohhhh daaaaaaamn!*" I heard everybody in the class groan at once.

"What that smell?" yelled Roland, squeezing his nose. "Why Patricia stankin' like a dead dog booty fart?"

The whole class fell out, pointing and cackling. I wanted to tell them it wasn't *my* funk they were smelling—it was Janice's socks stinking up the place. I was getting attacked over a case of mistaken funk identity, but they were laughing so loud there wasn't nothing I could do to set the record straight. The teacher was tee-heeing right along with the rest of them. She tried to hide it, but I could see her snickering as she sprayed air freshener all around her desk.

After that, those kids treated me even worse than before. They called me Funk Box, Hot Foot, Fish Feet, Stank Machine, and Pussy Foot Patricia. I felt so rotten, I just wanted to disappear. A few years later, when I got pregnant in the eighth grade, I made a vow to my baby that I'd never let her out in the world looking like nobody cared about her at home.

Michael didn't know any of this because I never told him about Janice. He didn't know I had dirty-clothes PTSD, or that my childhood trauma meant I'd spend every last cent I had to make sure my kids were always clean and looking sharp. I didn't understand Michael's concerns about money, and he didn't know my fears. Instead, we argued about that Macy's bill like this was just another case of *bitches be shopping* and *husbands be getting mad*.

"This can't happen again," Michael said, looking angrier than I'd ever seen him. He took out a pair of scissors, cut the Macy's card in half, and threw it in the trash. He really thought he was doing something with that. But the next day, I picked up the phone and called Macy's. I made my voice sound deep, like a man. I reported that my card got damaged, and I needed them to mail me a replacement. "And while you're at it," I said, "I want to add my wife as an authorized user." If Michael wasn't able to understand *my* emergencies, I figured I needed an emergency credit card of my own.

Ten days later, my new Macy's card arrived in the mail. It was as easy as that.

In those days, like a lot of working mothers, I wasn't taking good care of myself. It was hard to find the time. I also didn't have the funds. With six kids, there was no extra money for me to get my hair done. I couldn't even afford the nail salon. Before Michael, I didn't have these problems. With all that dope money rolling in, I was always buying myself new clothes.

I had jeans and tops and hoodies and jackets piled on chairs and the sofa and spilling out of bags on the floor. I rocked Guess, Ralph Lauren, Karl Kani, Tommy Hilfiger, Polo, FUBU, Puma, and Cross Colours. I could get my hair done anytime I pleased. I missed the freedom of buying whatever whenever I wanted. I missed that good feeling I had when I was dressed nice and looked sharp.

I'm not a vain person. But after we moved to Riverdale, some days I'd look in the mirror and barely recognize the woman staring back at me. It got even worse after I had our two babies back-to-back. I was carrying extra weight, and all I could fit into was Michael's old T-shirt and my stretched-out baggy sweats. I wore my hair in a little pony tied with a rubber band. It was the lowest I'd felt about myself in years.

To me, this was a mental health emergency. I needed to do something for me. So I went off to Macy's with my emergency credit card—the card Michael didn't even know I had.

I bought a cute pair of wedge heels. And a denim vest. And a pocketbook to match the shoes. It was a good start. But it wasn't a full outfit. Macy's didn't have a great selection of plus-size women's clothes. I needed to go to Lane Bryant, where they specialize in fashion for big girls like me.

Just like Macy's, Lane Bryant had its own in-store credit card. I filled out an application using Michael's Social Security number. A few weeks later, a Lane Bryant retail card arrived in the mail. At the store, I tried on tops and pants in every color. I slid my girls into one of them forty-two-dollar extra-support bras. I turned to the side and admired my new perky reflection. It was like the sun shining through the clouds after a rainstorm. Finally, I had a little joy in my life! *You deserve it*, I told myself as I left the store with a bulging shopping bag. It felt so good to do something for myself that I kept going back for more.

A few months later when I couldn't find a top I liked at Lane Bryant, I used Michael's information to get an in-store credit card for Ashley Stewart. Now I had three cards he didn't know about and a whole system to keep my secret.

After a shopping expedition, I'd hide my new clothes in the back of the kids' closet and slide my new shoes under the bed. I always made sure I got home before Michael so I could check the mailbox for bills. If I found one, I'd rip it up and throw it in the trash.

I did everything to cover my tracks. But credit card companies are like the mob. If you owe them money, they'll hunt you down. One afternoon when I wasn't home, some muthafucka from Macy's called. Michael picked up the phone. The person on the other end of the line informed him that not only was his payment three months overdue, but that the card was also maxed out. Michael told the lady there had to be a mistake. "I *used to* have a Macy's card," he'd told her. "But I cut it up, so I don't have one anymore." The billing department lady started listing off the charges. That's when Michael knew that the charges had come from me. By the time I got home, he was fuming. "You went behind my back," he said.

I tried to explain that these were all emergencies. "Oh really," he said. "What kind of 'emergency' needs a pocketbook and new shoes?"

A few weeks later, things only got worse when Michael got to the mailbox before I had a chance to throw away the bills. "Who the hell is Lane Bryant?" he wanted to know. "And why do I owe him all this damn money?"

The next few years were like a slow-rolling disaster. I kept getting new credit cards and Michael kept finding out that he owed money on cards he didn't even know he had. All we did was fight.

We didn't agree on how to spend money. We were even further apart when it came to managing debt. Michael thought it was important for us to pay what we owed. I didn't see the point.

Growing up, I learned there are two types of debt: one you took seriously, the other everybody ignored.

The first type of debt included all hood business transactions: drug deals, the numbers man, buying stuff on credit at the corner store. If you didn't pay off those debts, you'd get your ass stomped for sure. When I was in the streets, I watched one drug dealer shoot another in the gut over an unpaid debt. I saw a different dealer get stabbed in his eye when he tried to walk out on a tab. At my granddaddy's liquor house, all the customers knew that he kept a baseball bat behind the bar and a loaded .38 Special tucked in the waistband of his pants. He'd fuck you up both ways if you tried to mess with his money. Where I come from, you don't mess around when you owe money to independent entrepreneurs.

Every other money-owing situation—traffic tickets, utility bills, or back rent for the landlord—wasn't nothing you needed to worry about. I learned that lesson when I was fifteen and pregnant with baby number two.

By then, I'd moved out of Mildred's efficiency and was living on my own. My welfare was two hundred thirty-five dollars a month. I was struggling to come up with the rent. My new neighbor, Roxie, must have sensed I was in trouble, because one morning she sat me down and schooled me on hood financial management.

"Girl," she said, taking a slow drag from the Kool dangling off her lip, "don't even worry about them landlords." She explained that I could stay in the apartment without paying rent until the sheriff showed up to evict my ass. "That shit can take months," Roxie said. That was some of the stupidest advice I've ever heard. But at the time, I didn't know any better. I'd seen my own mama do the same thing. I thought everybody lived that way.

In Riverdale, I tried to explain my thinking to Michael. "You don't need to pay this," I said when he flashed a credit card bill in my face. "You think Lane Bryant's gonna come to the house and repossess my bras?" I snatched the bill from his hand, ripped it up, and threw it in the trash. "You can't pay what you don't have."

Michael let out a sigh of exhaustion, shook his head, and walked away.

We fought, argued, and bickered about money. It went on and on and on. It was my fault. Not because of the shopping, but because I refused to listen when Michael tried to explain the problems I was causing. He'd start talking and I'd just tune him out. I wasn't even *trying* to understand his perspective. In all our years together, we'd never been so far apart. Something had to give.

One evening after the kids were in bed, I found Michael sitting at the kitchen table, his head in his hands, a stack of bills spread out around him. He glanced in my direction and turned back to the bills without saying a word. I saw the sadness in his eyes and felt a pain in my heart. It suddenly hit me: Michael had the weight of our family on his shoulders, and I wasn't doing anything to help carry the burden.

In fact, I was just making it worse. We were supposed to be partners, but I'd let him feel like he was all alone.

Michael had shown me nothing but love since the day we met. He took care of my kids and my sister's kids like they were his very own. He worked a good job. He put food on the table. He loved me like no one ever had before. And in return, I went behind his back, lying and scheming and running up his bills. The man I loved was the victim of financial crime, and I was the con artist who done it. I had to make things right.

I sat down at the table beside him and asked him to show me how bad things really were. For the first time, I didn't get defensive. I didn't cuss him out. I kept my mouth shut and my mind open.

He took out the Macy's bill first. "This is the dollar amount you spent on purchases," he said, pointing to a figure. "And this is the interest rate," he said, pointing to another. "When we don't pay the entire balance, the store charges us interest. If we pay the bill late, they charge us a late fee. The late fee gets added to the total, and they charge us interest on *that*. Even if you don't buy another thing," he added, "the amount we owe will keep growing until we pay the whole thing off."

No one had ever broken it down for me the way Michael did that night. I realized that credit card companies are just like drug dealers. They make all their money from folks who run up their debt chasing that shopping high.

Michael took out his checkbook and wrote Lane Bryant a check for thirty-five dollars, the minimum payment due. With half a dozen maxed-out credit cards to pay off, the minimum was all he could afford.

By 2006, we were thirty-five thousand dollars in credit card debt. Our marriage survived. But I'm pretty sure the stress of paying off that debt is how Michael lost all his hair.

CHAPTER 9

FUNNY LADY

One thing I know for sure: there's nothing funnier than the truth. Especially when that truth is something everybody is thinking but nobody will say out loud.

I learned this one afternoon at a football field in Riverdale, sitting in the bleachers with a bunch of other parents, watching our kids play ball. Everybody was complaining about the coach, who was more focused on giving his own son playing time than trying to win the damn game.

All the parents thought he was playing favorites. But I was the only one who called him out. "Sir, is you crazy?" I hollered from the sidelines. It was the top of the second quarter, and the coach had just put his little boy back on the field instead of giving another player a chance. That boy had Coke-bottle eyeglasses and zero peripheral vision. "Coach!" I yelled again. "What are you doing? Cuz it ain't working!"

The coach put his hands on his hips and glared in my direction, like he thought that would shut me up. But by then, I had a little audience. All the parents were wondering what I was going to say next. I didn't want to make the little boy feel bad. So I lowered my voice and started talking shit that only the parents could hear. "That child's not going to no NFL," I said. "Only place he headed is the optometrist. Coach got him out here *quarterbacking*. That little boy can't even see the damn ball." I heard folks tee-heeing all around me.

"Girl, you're hilarious," a mother named Tyra told me later that afternoon. Tyra had moved to Riverdale from New York. She was real smart, with two college degrees and a son who played football with Nikia. She and I became fast friends. "You're a natural-born entertainer," Tyra said that afternoon on the bleachers. "You're so funny. You should be doing stand-up."

It wasn't the first time I'd heard this. Not long after me and Michael moved to Riverdale, Ms. Campbell, my caseworker at the Positive Employment and Community Help Welfare-to-Work program, had also said I should be a comedian, which surprised the hell outta me. Because at the time, I was trying hard to make her cry.

I learned early in life that if a caseworker feels sorry for you, she'll pull some strings behind the scenes to help you get extra benefits. When I was about eight years old, I told Ms. Munroe, Mama's caseworker from the Division of Family and Children's Services, that Mildred had beat my ass with an extension cord. Ms. Munroe's eyes filled with tears. The next thing I knew, she hooked me up with free summer sleepaway camp. That camp fed us three meals a day. I went fishing and won a medal for archery. Best of all, I got to be out of Mama's house. On the first day of camp, Ms. Munroe even took me to the Kmart on Cleveland Avenue and bought me camp supplies: a swimsuit, some shorts and tops, a toothbrush, a comb, insect repellent, a sleeping bag, a washcloth, and a towel. Then she put me in her white Buick and drove me to the camp herself. That's the type of above and beyond I'd seen caseworkers do when I was young.

So when I met Ms. Campbell at the Welfare-to-Work program, I tried to pull on her caseworker heartstrings by telling her about my past.

"It hasn't been easy for me," I told her. "I was pregnant at thirteen. My baby daddy was a piece of shit. That nigga beat me with a roller skate and then shot me in the head."

Ms. Campbell gasped in shock.

"Yes, ma'am," I continued. "Hand to Black Baby Jesus, I'm not lying. I also got shot in the left areola. One of my crackhead customers came running down the street with a pistol and blew my nipple straight off. And I got hit by a dump truck."

"Oh my goodness," she said, her eyes growing wide.

"It's okay," I told her. "I only need one nipple. God gave me a spare."

I thought I saw a flicker of a smile pass Ms. Campbell's lips, which was not the reaction I was going for. So I started telling her about Mildred, thinking for sure that would make her cry.

"My mama was so mean," I told the caseworker. "If I didn't fix her gin and water just the way she liked it, she'd take out her .22 and fire that pistol right inside the house. I had a *real* bad childhood," I repeated. "Other kids were at the rec center playing hopscotch and I was at home dodging strays."

Ms. Campbell looked down at her lap as though she was examining a speck of dust. I noticed her shoulders shaking. I couldn't believe it; I'd told her my sob stories and she was cracking up.

"I'm sorry, Patricia," she said, covering her mouth with her hand. "I don't mean to chuckle, but you are a wonderful storyteller. You've turned your pain into something funny. The way you find humor in difficult times is truly a gift from God."

At my next appointment, I told her more sad stories. She giggled so much, I thought she was gonna fall right out of her chair. That's when she asked if I'd ever thought about trying stand-up comedy.

"Girl, you remind me of Richard Pryor," she said. "A gift like yours is meant to be shared."

Before that conversation, I didn't even know that Richard Pryor did stand-up. I only knew him from the movies. And I sure as hell didn't know that comedy could be a career.

Across the hall from Ms. Campbell's office was an employment center for welfare recipients in search of a job. Along the back wall was a row of computers. I looked up "Richard Pryor" to see what kinda money this nigga made. But this was before Google and celebrity net worth websites. All I found were fan pages listing Pryor as the greatest stand-up comic of all time.

At home that night, I asked Michael if he knew anything about stand-up comedy. "How much you think a person gets paid for doing something like that?" I asked.

"You know that show *Seinfeld*?" Michael said. "He started as a stand-up. That's how he's got his own TV show. Now he's a multi-millionaire. So I guess if you're Jerry Seinfeld funny, you can get rich from telling jokes."

I'd never watched *Seinfeld* before I met Michael. That show was just another thing he introduced into my life, along with voting in local elections and tipping 20 percent. I didn't expect a show about a goofy white dude and his weird-ass New York friends to be funny to me. But *Seinfeld* was hilarious. That's how I learned that a good comedian doesn't need to come from the same lifestyle as the audience. If a comic is talented, they can make anybody laugh.

I thought about Ms. Campbell, Tyra, and all those parents cracking up at Little League football week after week. I thought about Richard Pryor finding humor in his hardship. And I thought about having my own TV show and becoming a millionaire. I wondered if maybe the comedy world had a place for me.

Back then, Atlanta had two big comedy clubs: the Punchline, in Sandy Springs, where comics like Jeff Foxworthy and Larry the Cable Guy performed; and Uptown Comedy Corner, in Buckhead, that featured "urban" acts.

"Urban" is the code word club bookers use when what they really mean is "Black." Atlanta is in the Deep South, and the comedy scene could be pretty segregated—not by law, but by culture. At the Punchline, you could find comics who proudly called themselves "rednecks" and did material about . . . hell, I don't know what the fuck jokes comics told over there. Meanwhile, folks like Sommore, Rickey Smiley, and Earthquake headlined weekend shows at Uptown.

The city also had a mess of smaller, hole-in-the-wall spots where amateur comics and up-and-comers had a chance to perform any night of the week. These weren't real comedy clubs. They were bars, restaurants, lounges, even art galleries that once a week would stick a mic stand on a riser and put on a little comedy show, with a local comic as the host. Comedians call these spots "workout rooms" because it's where we go to work out new material. But not all rooms are the same.

In spots where it's mostly white folks, the audience will sit quietly and give a stand-up time to get into their groove. In Black rooms—where pretty much everybody onstage and most of the audience is Black—folks don't have that type of patience. You gotta hit hard and fast with your punch lines. If you don't get a good laugh in the first three and a half seconds, the crowd will jingle their car keys, yell "You suck!" and boo your ass right off the stage. I've heard white comics telling stories about "that one time" they played a Black room. They talk about it like they survived the war.

Black rooms are like comedy boot camps—only the strong survive. But I was ready for shit; I grew up in a war zone. I got heckled all day every day by a bunch of mean-as-hell little-kid bullies at school. It was impossible for me to whoop all they asses at once. So I learned how to fight back with my words. In Atlanta, we called it jonesing. Some folks call it roasting. For me, it was self-defense. Anybody so much as looked at me sideways and I'd read them, they mama, daddy, sister, brother, pastor, *and* they pet dog to filth. Anybody could get it. I had the fastest mouth at Dean Rusk Elementary. I discovered that if I could get a group of kids laughing at whoever was bothering me that day, the bully would leave me alone. Black rooms didn't scare me. I'd been training for that shit all my life.

After Ms. Campbell told me I had a special gift, I started hitting up comedy spots around Atlanta to check out the local scene. I saw a whole lotta men who thought they was funny talking about "bitches be trippin'" or "my wife be trippin'" or making jokes about how fat girls will cook you a whole-ass meal at three o'clock in the morning. That shit made me so mad. Because who the hell is getting out of bed to cook for a nigga just because she's fat? I heard that shit and thought, *I'm way funnier than this.*

One Tuesday night, I put on a nice outfit, picked up my friend Melany, and went to a spot in Morrow, Georgia, for a comedy open mic night. I put my name on the sign-up sheet and whispered to Melany, "If this shit don't work out, you better not tell nobody we was here."

My name was called, and I felt my heart pounding out my chest as I made my way to the stage. I looked out at the room full of people and realized I had to do something to grab their attention, because it looked like none of them was even listening. There were a couple of drunks sitting at the bar sipping on Henny, and one of them was half asleep. Off to the left, a young boy—probably a college student from Clayton State—was busy trying to holler at a chick sitting at the next table. In the front row, a man and woman were having a heated-ass argument—talking about "No, you didn't" and "Yes, I did, bitch"—like they was in the privacy of their own home.

"Hey y'all," I said, grabbing the mic and praying not to bomb. "My name is Ms. Pat."

I didn't know anything about setups or punch lines. I just started talking. I told a story about my brother Andre, who thought he was a criminal mastermind. "He's a cat burglar," I said. "Like Garfield in a durag."

That got a laugh. I kept on going. From the corner of my eye, I noticed the college boy had stopped talking to the girl and was now watching me onstage. "During the holidays, he'll take all y'all Christmas presents from under the tree," I continued. "He calls himself Nigga Claus." The whole room busted out laughing.

I stepped off the stage to a round of applause and felt a rush of excitement I'd never felt before. I wanted to turn around, get right back on that stage, and do it again. That shit was electrifying; I wanted more, more, more. If this was how my sister felt every time she hit that pipe, then I guess I understand her addiction.

I started hitting up comedy spots a couple of times a week after that. I always took a friend like Tyra or Melany with me for moral support. Eventually, I started making friends with Atlanta comics, like Dirty South, Double D, and Kourtlyn.

One night, about a year after I started performing, Double D told me to meet him at Cobalt Lounge for a comedy night hosted by local comic Arlen "Griff" Griffin. Griff cohosted a radio show on Hot 107.9 and would promote his comedy night on the air. I walked in and saw that the room was packed with at least a hundred and fifty people, which was about a hundred more people than I'd ever performed in front of before.

Double D said it would be a good room for me to get up and do a set. But I was so nervous, I told him no. "I can't tonight," I said. "My period just came on." I sounded like I was trying to get out of gym class. Double D just laughed. He didn't bother to tell me that he'd already put my name on the list. I only found out I was performing when I heard Griff call me to the stage.

"Damn you, nigga," I said to Double D, laughing to hide my nerves.

"You can't be no comic if you're scared to get up," he said with a shrug.

I stepped onstage, put a big smile on my face, and grabbed the mic. "How y'all doing?" I said. "I'm Ms.—"

I didn't even get my name out my mouth when a corny-ass dude in the front row, dressed in a gray turtleneck sweater with a dog design on the front, stood up and whipped a Nerf ball at my head like he was pitching for the Atlanta Braves. It happened so quick, I didn't even have time to duck.

It turns out that in addition to signing me up without my consent, Double D had also neglected to mention that before the show, Griff had handed audience members foam Nerf balls with instructions to throw them at any comic if they didn't like a joke. In Black rooms, folks threw all kinds of shit at the stage when they didn't like a comic. It ain't nothing to see lemon wedges, balled-up paper napkins, car keys, chicken wings, or ketchup packets flying through the air. Griff must have gone out and bought a bulk order of Nerf balls. He thought his gimmick for the night was hilarious. It sure as shit wasn't funny to me.

When that Nerf ball hit my face, it was like a switch flipped inside me. I went from stand-up comic to who-the-fuck-you-think-you-is-because-I-will-beat-yo'-muthafucking-ass-I'm-from-the-streets-bitch faster than a blink of an eye.

"Nigga!" I hollered at the man who popped me. "You must lost yo' damn mind. Look at him," I said to the crowd. "He got on a turtleneck. Y'all, let's rob this nigga!" For five straight minutes, I roasted his ass to a crisp. I clowned him for his corny-ass sweater, his fucked-up grill, and the fact that he was dressed up for date night with no woman in sight. "She seen this nigga's sweater and canceled," I said. "You look like your shirt be choking you out." I wasn't trying to be funny; I was mad as hell. But I had that room howling.

Sometimes, when a female comic calls out a man from the stage, he'll rise up and start heckling from the audience, trying to show everybody who's boss. One night, when I was out with Tyra, I got into it with a dude who wouldn't stop playing pool while I was trying to do my set. "Sir, do I come on your job and make a whole bunch of noise while you working?" I asked, hoping that would shut him up.

He yelled back, "Bitch, you ain't even funny." That pissed me off. So I tore his ass up.

"You rude as hell, and you got the nerve to be a lil' short-ass nigga, too," I said, laughing. He got madder and madder.

"Keep going, bitch," he sneered. "I got something for yo' ass."

I looked over at Tyra sitting in the front row, her eyes as wide as saucers. Judging by his stone face, whatever BaldHead had for me sure as hell wasn't nothing nice.

I finished my set, jumped offstage, and power walked my ass out the club. Tyra was already waiting in the getaway car. "Girl," she said, shaken. "I thought he was finna blow your brains out. I was getting ready to meet my maker."

BaldHead wanted to fight me. But Turtleneck was a different type; he didn't have not one single retort. He just sat there looking stupid.

I didn't tell a single joke from my set that night. I still got a standing ovation.

Before I started doing comedy, I'd done a lot of jobs in my life. I flipped burgers at McDonald's and Burger King, stocked shelves at Target, rang up customers at Walmart, and worked the line at GM. But in all those positions, I was always serving someone else's plan and lining someone else's pocket. When I got into stand-up, it reminded me that I wasn't built to be nobody's employee. I have that independent, entrepreneurial spirit. I need to be my own boss. At open mics, I wasn't making money, but I was in charge of product development, quality control, and customer relations, just like back in the day when I was on the block selling dope.

To get good at comedy takes a lot of practice. I tried to get onstage as often as I could. But we had eight kids, two of them still in preschool. Some nights, it was impossible for me to get out of the house. Then, in 2004, everything changed.

Sweetie called the house one afternoon, telling me she wanted her daughters back. "I'm they mama," she said. "They need to be with me."

"No, they sure as hell don't," I said, slamming down the phone. Sweetie thinking she was fit to raise those girls was the dumbest shit I ever heard.

For almost ten years, Michael and I had been the only parents those girls could depend on. We'd done everything for them. They were thriving in school and sports. One year, LaDontay's track team made it into the Junior Olympics. The meet was in Florida. Me and Michael worked a whole lot of overtime to make sure she could go.

On our last day of the trip, we took the kids to Universal Studios so they could go on some rides. Admission was $49.95 per person.

With everything we'd already spent on gas, food, and the hotel bill, the amusement park admission wiped us out. We had to drive back to Atlanta in the middle of the night just so the kids couldn't tell us they were hungry and ask us to stop for food.

Me and Michael didn't have a lot. But there wasn't nothing we wouldn't do for those girls. They had a damn good life with us.

I don't know how Sweetie convinced a judge that she was off drugs and fit to parent. But she was a world-class liar. I guess she conned the judge at family court. Not long after that phone call, she showed up at our house with the cops and took her girls away.

I was so mad. What kind of system would snatch children out of a loving home and send them straight to the fiery pits of hell with their crack addict mama? "Everyone deserves a second chance," Michael said. "You never know how things might turn out." But I knew my sister. That crackhead wasn't never going to get her shit together. Sweetie was as bad as our mama.

I cried for weeks after Sweetie took her girls. I missed them so bad, I could barely stand to be at home. The house was too damn quiet. I needed to take my mind off my troubles. That's when I started going out to do comedy seven nights a week.

There were so many places to perform in Atlanta, I'd hit up two, sometimes three spots a night. One time, I did a ten-minute set in some dude's living room. All that practice paid off. After a while, I got so good that I could step onstage in an ice-cold room where not one damn person was laughing and heat that bitch up so folks were rolling on the floor. Soon, I didn't even have to put my name on sign-up sheets. When I walked into a spot, the emcee would call out, "Hey y'all, Ms. Pat's in the house." If I wanted to go up, they'd put me right onstage.

I started getting recognized out in the real world, too. In the cereal aisle at Kroger, a lady I'd never seen before called out my name. "Ms. Pat, you funny as hell," she said. "Girl, you finna be a star. I can tell!"

At the ripe old age of thirty-two, I'd finally found my calling, my passion, my path in life. In Atlanta's comedy scene, I had a future. People knew my name.

I was so sure that things were moving in the right direction, I went online and bought a URL domain for my comedy website, even though I didn't have no shit to post there. I'd noticed that every successful comic had a website. When destiny called, and I became a successful comic too, I needed to be ready to claim my place.

I don't know why I was so confident that I'd make it. I knew plenty of comics who'd been grinding for a decade or more who were *still* waiting for their big break. At night, I'd lie in bed with visions of my future dancing in my head: there I am, my name in lights on the marquee of a big theater; there I am onstage, making thousands of people laugh, and there I am on TV, starring in my very own show.

I was sure that the lady in the cereal aisle had been right. I *was* gonna be a star!

Then, thanks to General Motors, all my plans came tumbling down.

CHAPTER 10

STAGE BLOCKED

I'm going to be putting together transmissions," Michael said, telling me about the GM plant where he'd soon be working, which was three states away, in Indiana. I didn't want to move. But we had to.

For four years, Michael had been working full-time at General Motors, putting together minivans. He had a good salary and benefits, including Blue Cross Blue Shield insurance for the kids. But in 2008, GM closed down the Doraville plant. Some folks took buyouts or early retirement. But Michael was only thirty-six years old; he wanted to keep working. The company offered to relocate him to another GM facility, but the available jobs were all out of state.

If we *had* to move, I told Michael, the least he could do was keep us in the South. GM's Texas plant was an option, but Michael pointed out that the Texas facility assembled Escalades. He didn't want to work on those big-ass vehicles. His body was already breaking down.

GM pays well. But everybody who works the line knows that sooner or later the job will fuck you up. Michael's sister-in-law Betty needed surgery on her leg, her wrist, and her shoulder from injuries she got on the job. My niece ended up blowing out both her knees. Michael had come down with degenerative arthritis in his elbow. He wanted a GM job that involved less lifting, twisting, and wrenching his body and more time sitting on his ass. When he found out GM made Allison transmissions at their plant in Indianapolis, Michael signed up for the transfer.

I was so mad. I didn't want to live in no place that had snow. So I went online, logged into Michael's employee portal, and changed his selection from Indianapolis to Dallas. Then Michael did me dirty. He not only changed his choice *back* to Indianapolis; he also changed his password and locked me out of the system. "It's my job," he said. "My choice."

For the first time in our relationship, Michael was making a big decision that I didn't agree with and telling me I didn't have a say. He was paying all the bills. I didn't have a leg to stand on.

On a cloudy December day, we packed up our children and all our possessions and moved to Plainfield, Indiana, a suburb of Indianapolis and the whitest place I'd ever seen. Every house in the cookie-cutter subdivision looked the same, with gabled roofs and cream-colored siding. Even the mailboxes were identical. When Michael backed up over our mailbox by accident, we had to order the exact same model with the exact same lettering. It took so long for the new mailbox to arrive, I thought the homeowners' association was going to burn a cross in our front yard for messing with the neighborhood aesthetics.

"I hate it here," I said to Michael the day we moved into our new place. I told him the same thing every day afterward, for months. Plainfield had good schools for the kids. It was clean and safe, and the neighbors seemed friendly. But moving to this boring-ass suburb was unbearable for me. I didn't have any friends. There was not one soul food restaurant to eat at. When I wanted to get my hair done, I had to drive seven hours back to Atlanta. *That's* how white Plainfield was.

The hardest part about moving was that it knocked my comedy career right off the tracks. In Atlanta, I felt like I was *somebody*. It wasn't only that I was getting recognized in the cereal aisle. Atlanta comics also knew who I was. I'd made my way into the inner circle, which meant I had access to inside information about things like TV auditions or comedy contests. I was even getting invited out on the road to open for other performers. In Atlanta, my career was beginning to take off. In Indianapolis, nobody in the local comedy scene had ever heard of me before.

I knew I needed to start back at square one. But I felt so defeated, I didn't even want to try. All I did was sleep and cry and call my friends back in Atlanta and cry to them some more. I'm not a depressed person. But every day, my spirit sank a little lower. It was Michael who finally lit the fire under my ass that got me back in the game.

He came home from work one evening and found me boo-hooing on the sofa. "I fuckin' hate it here," I said for the millionth time. "I want to go back home."

"Okay," he responded with a shrug. "If that's what you really want, nobody's stopping you. You can give up and go back to Atlanta. Or," he added, "you can figure out a way to make this work."

Michael never yells. He don't like to argue. But when he thinks I'm making a mistake, he'll just say something real matter-of-fact that turns my whole perspective upside down. That's what happened the night he told me I could "give up" and move back to Atlanta.

I'd been complaining about Plainfield from the day we moved in. But when I heard Michael say "give up," it didn't sit right with me. It made me feel like a quitter. That's not me at all.

"Ain't nobody giving up," I told him. I promised myself that one day I'd find a way to move the family back home. But in the meantime, I was gonna prove to Michael, myself, and the universe that I could make it in this mayonnaise-eating town.

The next morning, I went online and searched "comedy clubs near me." The first spot I checked out was One-Liners in Greenwood, Indiana, about a thirty-five-minute drive from where we lived. Walking into One-Liners was like going back in time. The place was dark and dingy, with old-fashioned wooden chairs and the smell of stale cigarette smoke hanging low in the air. One chilly Wednesday night, I took a seat near the back of the club to see what their open mic night was like. I got a crash course on what white people think is funny.

The first dude to go up did five minutes on how he lived in his parents' basement. The next guy talked about how his mama still made his bed. The third guy told a long, winding story about his pet cat and her hairballs. The fourth dude also had a story about a cat. The fifth comic, a young white woman with giant wire-rimmed glasses, told some jokes about her bird. *What in the Noah's Ark am I listening to?* I wondered. In Atlanta, we didn't do this type of comedy. Plus, I don't understand why anybody likes cats. They are the sneakiest of all God's creatures, walking all over the kitchen counters with their nasty shitty-litter feet.

It wasn't only that the subject matter was different. The delivery, tempo, and vibe were unfamiliar, too. I was used to quick-fire comics who hit the audience hard and fast with joke after joke. But these Indiana comics would be wandering all over the damn place before they even thought about hitting a punch line. I kept expecting the audience to boo these amateurs right off the stage, but everybody in the room, except for me, looked like they were having fun.

I didn't feel comfortable in that club. But I needed a place to do comedy, so I had to figure this shit out. The next week, I went back to One-Liners and put my name on the list for open mic.

There were only a couple of dozen people in the club that night. One dude, dressed in a button-down work shirt and blue tie, looked nervous as hell, like maybe he was there only because his friends from work had dared him to try stand-up. At the next table, a skinny dude with bright-red hair was staring hard at his notebook, which I figured was probably filled with stories about his cats. I looked around and noticed that I was the only Black person in the room.

Onstage, I introduced myself, explaining that I'd recently moved from Atlanta.

"I live down in Plainfield," I said with a big smile. "Y'all know where that is? Boy, that shit can't get no whiter." I talked about the culture shock of having a neighbor show up at my door with a homemade chocolate cake. "I have diabetes. I thought she was tryna kill me." Then I did a bit about driving around the area with a real estate agent, looking for a place to live: "So I'm staring out the window and I said to him, 'Sir, we can't live out here. These people don't cut their grass!' He looked at me like I was crazy. He says, 'Ma'am, that isn't grass . . . that's *corn*.'"

I guess those folks got a kick out of hearing a Black woman from the inner city making jokes about their agriculture, because I got some good laughs that night. I went back the following Wednesday, put my name on the list, and did it again. Pretty soon, I was a regular at One-Liners' open mic.

The way comedy clubs work is that if a new comic kills over and over at open mic, the club will give that comic a chance to emcee in front of a paying crowd. At One-Liners, it only took me a couple of months before Scott, the manager, gave me a shot to host the weekend shows.

The pay was only thirty dollars a night. But I wasn't doing this for the money. One-Liners had a hundred-and-twenty-five-seat capacity. On the weekends, practically every seat would be filled. At open mics, I was only performing in front of twenty or thirty people. Hosting a weekend show gave me a hundred and twenty-five chances to win a hundred and twenty-five new fans.

Before my first gig, Scott pulled me aside. "Remember, this is the early crowd," he said. "So no salty language and nothing *explicit*."

I stared back at him, confused. My material wasn't explicit. I used to have a sex joke: "You ever sucked a man's dick so long you got cotton mouth?" But that was back when I was starting out. I hadn't told that joke in years. Plus, I'd heard enough cat and bird material to know that at One-Liners dirty jokes weren't the vibe.

"No cursing," he clarified. "Keep it clean."

"I can do a show with no cussing," I assured him. "That's not a fucking problem." I gave him a big smile to let him know he had nothing to worry about with me.

My job was to warm up the audience with about ten minutes of my own material, then introduce each act and bring them up onstage. I did good that night. I got the crowd in a laughing mood, just like I was supposed to. When the headliner took the stage, the audience was nice and toasty. Scott liked what he saw and asked me to host again the next weekend. He only had one complaint: he said I went over my time.

Time is a big thing in comedy clubs. Every stand-up is given a set number of minutes to perform—the opener might get ten minutes; the feature act gets about twenty; and the headliner does around forty-five. As the emcee, I could do ten minutes of my own material. Then I was supposed to introduce the opener and get the hell off the stage. To keep folks on time, most clubs have a red light on the back wall that the manager flicks on and off at the one-minute mark, letting the person onstage know they need to wrap it up.

When a comic runs the light, some folks think it's like "stealing" from another comic's time. But I'd cut my teeth doing comedy in Black rooms in Atlanta. Those places didn't have no red light. It was more of a *whatever goes* situation. The same audience that would boo your ass offstage if you weren't funny would want you to stay up there and keep going if you were doing good. There was no time limit on being funny.

At One-Liners, I got plenty of laughs while hosting, so I didn't think it made sense for me to rush right offstage. I only went over my time by one or two, maybe four or five, minutes. At most, I did an extra seven—but that's only because I had folks cracking up.

The first night I ran the light, Scott gave me a warning. The second time, he got mad. The third time, we got into an argument. I told him I *was* being "professional" and "respectful." I said I was only trying to put on a good show. Scott told me not to come back.

Fine, I thought. *I didn't like your run-down club and your cat-loving comics anyway.*

The next day, I started looking for another club to call home.

Crackers Comedy Club was in an area called Broad Ripple, on the north side of Indianapolis. The club had been around since the 1980s. It was above a restaurant. The whole place smelled like old popcorn.

The first time I went to open mic at Crackers, I discovered the club had a rule that each comic could only perform at one open mic night per month. That might be fine for amateurs. But this wasn't no little side hobby for me. I wasn't about to stick around at a club that made me wait an entire month for another chance to get back onstage.

In Indianapolis, there was one more comedy club left to try.

Morty's Comedy Joint had been open less than a year and was already gaining a reputation as the hottest spot in town. The space had brighter stage lighting, a better sound system, and a more modern feel than Crackers. When stand-ups like Ralphie May, Sheryl Underwood, and Jeffrey Ross came to town, they headlined Morty's on the weekend.

I showed up on a Tuesday night for open mic, wrote my name

on the sign-up sheet, and waited for Jack, the club's manager, talent booker, and emcee for the evening, to call me to the stage.

"We got another female coming up," Jack said, introducing me. He was a short-ass round dude, barely taller than me, with a big head and no neck, looking like a Teletubby. As soon as I heard him speak, I thought, *This corny-ass nigga sounds like he don't have a single Black friend.*

"How about that, ladies?" Jack continued. "A little estrogen in the house. Give a big round of applause for Ms. Pat!"

I stepped onstage, flashing a smile. "Hey, white people!" I said.

I opened with the story about my new neighbors bringing me homemade cakes. Then I did a bit about looking through Michael's phone and finding a number saved for "K.K." and dialing the number to see if he was cheating. "A woman answered," I told the crowd. "She goes, 'Thank you for calling Krispy Kreme.'" I finished my set with some jokes about how my plus-size daughter was the wrong size for getting kidnapped. "When's the last time you seen a fat kid on the back of a milk carton?" I asked. "That's right, *never*. They too heavy to lift!" That crowd must have been starved for comedy, because they gave me a standing ovation. I thought to myself, *Morty's might be my place.*

After me, a young comic named Deon Curry went up.

"Damn," he said, taking the mic. "I wish my mama was that funny." Deon was tall and slim, and I wasn't expecting him to be any good, because he was only twenty-one. But he told a story about his brother having a baby with his white girlfriend. He described the baby shower, where all the white folks huddled on one side of the room, and the Black folks all showed up late. "It looked like a Mississippi bus line from nineteen fifty-five," he said. "There was a fireman with a hose and a German shepherd, and everyone was uncomfortable." That shit had me *howling*. After his set, I told Deon, "You real funny." He said the same back to me.

The only person who *didn't* seem to like either of us was Jack, Morty's manager, which turned out to be a very big problem.

After my first time at Morty's, I started showing up every Tuesday for open mic. I'd try out new material, throw in a couple of jokes that always killed in Atlanta, and do some crowd work, ad-libbing from the stage.

One Tuesday night, a young dude came in with a bunch of friends and signed up for open mic. He was dressed ridiculous, in sagging jeans and a white T-shirt so big it looked like a nightgown. I don't know how this young man got past the doorman, because that boy didn't look old enough to vote. When his name was called, he got onstage and told a Kevin Hart joke. First of all, everybody knows that you do not do other people's material. Second, he didn't even tell the joke right. After his Kevin Hart impersonation bombed, the boy got all flustered and started rambling, talking shit to everybody in the room. He was roasting the people he came in with and people in the audience that he didn't even know. He wasn't telling jokes. He was just cussing people out. Then he got to me.

I was sitting at a table about four rows back from the stage. He pointed in my direction and started laughing. "Look at this fat bitch, here!" he said. That was his first mistake, because I don't like being called none of them words, not "fat," not "bitch," and definitely not "look at this."

I told Jack to put me up next. "I'm sorry about that little boy up here tryna act like he's somebody," I told the crowd. Then I started apologizing to everyone he'd just insulted. "Baby," I said to a pregnant lady sitting at a back table with her girlfriends. "Don't pay this little muthafucka no mind. I'm sure you *do* know who your baby daddy is. And if you don't, that's okay. This ain't the *Maury* show." Then I turned to the young man who'd created this mess and started going in on *him*. "Look here," I said, "you fake-ass wannabe Kevin Hart. How dare you come in here tryna do somebody else joke. *And* fuck it up? The only thing you got in common with Kevin is your size. You a small-ass nigga, but you big on not being funny."

I guess being chewed out in front of his friends made him feel some type of way, because he jumped out of his seat and started throwing up gang signs. "You think you hard?" I asked, laughing. "I'm from Atlanta, Georgia, *bitch*. You don't scare me."

"Keep talking!" he hollered. "I'ma come up there and fuck your fat ass up."

"I *dare* you to come up here," I said. "Baby, *please* come on. You don't know who the fuck you playin' with." I made it clear that I was not the one, the two, *or* the three. But this dumbass marched right up on that stage. The next thing I knew, the two of us were throwing hands, brawling like we was auditioning for the WWE.

He tried to get me in a headlock. I swung him like a rag doll. The two of us went flying offstage; my body went in one direction, and my wig sailed the other way, landing right in Deon's strawberry daiquiri. It took three people, including Deon, to peel me and that boy apart.

From the corner of my eye, I could see Jack standing in the back of the room. He had his arms crossed and his face screwed up in a scowl. The way he was shaking his head, he looked like one of those school principals who expel kids for having too much fun.

I don't know why he was so salty. Nobody got hurt that night, except my wash-'n'-go wig. I had to put her in a plastic sack so she wouldn't drip daiquiri on my car seat on my drive home.

I hadn't planned on getting in a stage fight, but that shit *was* funny. Folks were laughing about it for weeks. Deon said watching my sets was like riding a roller coaster. "It's exciting," he said. "But you also have this feeling like, *What the fuck is happening?*" I guess folks liked it. After a few months, I had a little buzz on my name. People even started calling Morty's just to see if I was performing. You'd think Jack would appreciate a comic with that type of appeal. But the more popular I became, the more he seemed to despise me. I think maybe Jack was jealous.

Like a lot of comedy club managers, Jack was also a stand-up—only I didn't think he was any good. He was stiff with his delivery. He had no charisma. He'd been doing comedy for more than a decade and seemed to fight for every laugh he got. I didn't have that problem. Neither did Deon. Audiences liked us. They thought we were funny. Every time we got onstage, it probably reminded Jack of just how much he sucked. Maybe that's why he treated me so mean.

I never did a single thing to that man. I didn't call him names. I didn't roast him in public. When I had shit to say about him, I always said it behind his back. But no matter how polite I was, it didn't make no difference. When I walked by, he'd mutter shit under his breath, like "Here she goes again." If a bunch of regulars was hanging out in the greenroom, he would walk away as soon as I started to speak. Jack was petty as hell. And not only to me. One time, the volume cut out in the middle of Deon's set. Jack said it was a "technical issue," but I think he did that shit on purpose. When other comics bought food or drinks at the club, Jack always gave them a discount. If me or Deon wanted something to eat, he made us pay full price. Jack never came right out and said he didn't like us, but the vibe was loud and clear.

If this was any other work situation, I would have said, "Fuck this," and walked out. When I was at McDonald's, my manager asked me to wipe down some tables that were already clean. It was a slow day. The place had been empty. I didn't appreciate her telling me to do shit for no good reason. I threw my hairnet on the floor, told her to kiss my ass, and bounced. I have a hot temper and low tolerance for bullshit and disrespect. But at Morty's, I had to suck it up. The only way for me to move my comedy career to the next level was to get more stage time. Jack was Morty's talent booker. That made him the stage gatekeeper.

I did everything I could to let him know I was serious about comedy. I performed at every open mic. I worked on new material. I showed up every weekend to study the headliners' sets. But anytime I asked him to let me host a weekend show, he'd shake his head and tell me no.

"Can you let me host a show this weekend?"

"You're not ready."

"How about next Friday?"

"Nope."

"Okay, but I'm available the weekend after that, if you need somebody."

"I won't."

For almost a year, I wouldn't leave that man alone. I was practically begging him to give me a chance. It was that important.

Emceeing weekend shows was more than just an opportunity to perform in front of a full house. It was also a chance to impress the headliner. If he or she liked my comedy, they might vouch for me with other club bookers or recommend me to other headliners looking for an opener.

I asked and asked and asked again for a chance to host. Finally, Jack said yes. "Just don't fuck it up," he said.

I was so excited. I drove seven hours to Atlanta to get my hair fixed, then borrowed Michael's credit card and bought myself new shoes and a hot-pink blouse so I'd look good onstage. I don't like to brag, but I think I did great on both the Friday and Saturday night shows. I warmed up the room. I didn't run the light. The crowd laughed at all my hey-white-people jokes.

If Jack liked me, it meant I would get to level up from open mic'er to emcee. He could start hiring me to host other shows. It might even become a regular thing. And then maybe I'd start getting booked for feature spots, too. I was finally making moves in my new city. All I needed was for Jack to say I did good.

But after the Saturday night show, when I asked him what he thought, he said, "I can't talk right now." For a solid week, he kept brushing me off. Finally, I cornered him one night when he was sitting alone at the end of the bar going through a stack of papers.

"How'd I do?" I asked again.

He stared at me hard and let out a long sigh. "Honestly," he said, "I don't think you're right for the early show. Your material is too . . ." He paused like he was trying to find the right word. "Too *ghetto*."

"Ghetto?"

"Yeah, I just don't think a Midwestern white audience is going to get you. Especially not the early crowd. Your material is just too . . . too . . . you know, it's too *Black*."

I've been called a lot of ugly names in my life. But to hear a Black man tell me I'm "too Black," with so much ugliness in his voice, shocked the shit outta me.

"You need more practice," Jack continued. "A lot more." He explained that for the next six months, he wasn't going to put me back onstage. He told me to "just stick to open mic."

For almost a year, I'd been kissing his ass, saying "please" and "thank you" and acting all types of fake and phony. But instead of giving me a shot to earn some money and develop my skills, he banned me from his stage.

"You okay?" he asked.

I smiled, told him I was great, and thanked him for the feedback. I held my head high as I walked out of the club to the parking lot. I slid into my car and turned on the radio. As the sound of

Whitney singing *Didn't we almost have it allllllllll* filled the air, I put my head in my hands and bawled.

I wondered if this had been Jack's plan all along. *Did this nigga set me up just so he could tear me down?* I've never killed a man, but sitting in my car that night, I had fantasies of making Jack my first homicide. That's how hurt I was.

Of all the challenges I'd had in my comedy career—moving to Indianapolis, learning a different culture, doing open mics with amateur comics who told stories about their cats—swallowing my anger over the way Jack treated me was the hardest thing I had to do.

I couldn't fight. I couldn't argue. I had no power in this situation. All I could do was be patient, which was not something I knew how to do.

I thought about how Michael moved through the world, slow and steady. At GM, he did his work and never cussed out his boss, because he knew if he stuck with it, at the end of thirty years, he'd get a pension. I never understood that about him. The way he was okay waiting for good things to come. That's never been me. I move fast. I'm restless and impatient. I don't know any other way to get shit done. But now, it seemed, if I wanted to become a successful comic, I needed more than skills onstage. I also needed to develop a whole new personality trait.

I needed to learn to wait.

CHAPTER 11

THURSDAY NIGHT SHOW

In Plainfield, I had a day job as a shift manager at Taco Bell. From ten in the morning until four in the afternoon, I sat at the drive-thru taking orders for Cheesy Gorditas and asking folks, "You want a drink with that?" At the end of my shift, I'd go home, eat dinner, talk to Michael and the kids, and then leave for my second job at Morty's, trying to get my ass back on that stage.

On my way to the club, I talked to God. "Dear Lord, it's me, your number one fan," I'd tell him. "I know you got a lot of shit going on, but I'm asking if you could please help me out. I promise I won't brawl onstage no more. I just need a chance to get back up."

After Jack told me I wasn't good enough, I made it my mission to be at Morty's whenever the club was open. Part of me wanted to show Jack that I wasn't going to give up just because he insulted me. I also figured that with all my praying, God might bless me with an opportunity to take the stage at any moment. I had to be there to grab it.

On Friday and Saturday nights, I'd sit at the back of the club, sipping on my full-price Coke and watching the headliners perform. On Tuesdays, I did open mic and worked out new material. The rest of the week, I'd sit at the bar and call people from the Morty's contact list, offering them free or discounted tickets to upcoming shows. Jack paid me ten dollars an hour.

I was spending so much time at the club that I became good friends with Avery, the operations manager. He had a round face like Santa Claus, with a jolly and generous spirit to match. I talked to Avery about all types of stuff: my comedy dreams and frustrations and how bad I wanted to whoop Jack's Teletubby ass. Sometimes I'd tell Avery stories about my messed-up childhood and all the crimes I'd done to get by.

I told him about living in Granddaddy's liquor house and how, when I was only six, Mildred would make me steal wallets from customers who got so drunk they passed out on the floor. I told him that Mildred used to beat the shit outta me but that she also didn't know how to read, so when she asked me to read her horoscope in the newspaper, I'd just make shit up. Like, "Sagittarius: this is not a good day to whoop your children." I told him that at Granddaddy's funeral my cousin's son lifted his left butt cheek and let out the loudest fart I ever heard. "His mama stood up and started whooping that boy from the rootie to the tootie, right there in the pews," I told Avery. "The minister didn't even stop the service!"

One night I told him how, when I was in sixth grade at Dean Rusk Elementary, my "boyfriend"—who was actually a grown-ass adult male sex predator—would drive by the school to pick me up, and not a damn person had shit to say about it. "When you twelve, your boyfriend is supposed to meet you after class on his *bicycle*," I said. "Not pull up to the schoolyard in no damn Chevy Nova."

Avery stared at me with wide eyes like he was watching a movie. Finally, he said, "You really need to put this stuff in your act." Now I was really confused. Jack said that audiences wouldn't "get" me because my material was too "ghetto," even though the spiciest joke in my set that weekend was about looking through Michael's phone and finding donuts. Jack made it sound like I needed to do cat jokes to get ahead in Indiana. But Avery was telling me the opposite. Instead of toning down my material, he thought I should lean in and tell true stories from my crazy life.

"You think folks is ready for all that?" I asked.

"Absolutely," he said. "As long as you make it funny."

I tried it out, adding a little story here and another there. I realized right away that some of my stories were too much for the crowd to take. One night, I got up and said, "So my deadbeat baby daddy shot me in the head."

"*Whoooa*," said a guy sitting in the front row. On the other side of the room, I heard a woman gasp. I had to reassure everybody, letting them know I was okay.

The next week, when I mentioned that I had my first baby at fourteen, I could feel the audience tighten up, like they didn't know how to react. "If you feel sorry for me," I said, "you can write me a check and we can cry about it together." That line broke the tension and got a laugh. That's how I learned that the hard truth would go down easier if I added a joke at the end of the story, like a pillow to soften the blow.

"So my baby daddy shot me in the head," I said at open mic the next week. "But it wasn't his fault, y'all. It was *my* fault because I ducked too slow." That got a few chuckles. But I could tell the crowd was still uneasy. So I worked on that tag for weeks, trying out different timing, where to pause and when to smile. Finally, I got it so I could talk about getting my scalp blown off and have a roomful of people crack up. Avery was right; audiences loved stories of domestic violence and attempted murder as long as I made them funny.

Sometimes, folks would come up to me after the show, grab my hands, and say things like, "I fuckin' love you." At first, it made me real uncomfortable. I wasn't raised with love and affection. When I hear kind words, it's hard for me to know what to believe. Then I realized it's usually not that deep. Most of the time, when folks say, "I love you," it just means they like my act. So I should probably just say, "Thank you," instead of "Love me? Nigga, we just met!" But I also found that when I talked about my personal life and childhood struggles, sometimes my comedy hit in ways I didn't expect.

One night, I was working out a new bit about getting pregnant in middle school. I told a story about my seventh-grade teacher showing us a drawing of a penis during health class: "So I put up my hand and said, 'Miss, I think you got that picture wrong. My baby daddy dick is way bigger than that.'"

After my set, I was hanging out in the lobby when a white woman approached me. She had one of those expensive haircuts that look like a high-end wig and a big-ass ring so bright it could blind you. She leaned in and whispered in my ear, "The same thing happened to me."

She said that she'd been molested as a child and had a baby at thirteen. "Keep doing what you're doing," she added. "Nobody talks about this stuff. People need to know the truth." She looked like the type of rich white lady who'd never talk to someone like me in real life. But here she was, sharing her deepest secret, telling me we were in the same messed-up club.

They say it takes a comic about ten years to find their voice and develop their own unique style. That's probably true. But after Avery encouraged me to tell my true stories, it felt like I was going through a total comedy transformation. Jack said I was only allowed to do open mics. But now that my comedy was becoming more honest and authentic, I wanted to get up in front of a weekend crowd even more.

I waited. I prayed. I honed my craft. I did my day shifts at Taco Bell, then drove to Morty's and prayed and waited some more.

Weeks and then months passed by. Then one day, God decided I'd suffered enough. He answered my prayer in the form of a giant winter blizzard that covered Chicago under a foot and a half of snow.

Morty's had a full house that night, packed from wall to wall. Even Mr. Roger, the club owner who lived out in New Jersey, came out to see the show. The night's headliner, D. L. Hughley, was driving in from Chicago. But with the storm, D. L. was running almost an hour late.

You can't just leave a paying audience staring at an empty stage. So Jack got up and did some of his own material. And as usual, he bombed. When he stepped off the stage, Mr. Roger nodded his head in my direction, telling Jack to put me up next. I'd been waiting for a chance. Now, here it was.

You got this, I told myself as I made my way to the stage. I opened with a few jokes about moving to Indiana. Then I started talking about being a mom. "So I had my kids young," I told the crowd. "Any of y'all had your kids young?" I paused and glanced around the room. "Like fifth or sixth grade?" That got a big laugh. The next jokes hit even harder. Pretty soon, I had that room on fire.

Just as I was finishing my set, I looked up and noticed D. L. Hughley had arrived and was standing in the back of the club watching me perform. At the end of the night, I was hanging out in the lobby with a bunch of local comics when D. L. approached me. "You're funny," he said.

"Thank you," I replied. It felt good to get a compliment from the headliner. What came next was even better. D. L.—one of the

Original Kings of Comedy—invited me to open for him at his four sold-out weekend shows.

"For real?" I asked.

"Absolutely."

For months, Jack had been gatekeeping the shit out of that stage. That gate was coming down.

Three months after the Chicago snowstorm, Jack offered me a regular hosting gig. I'm sure that shit ate him up inside, like swallowing battery acid. But I don't think he had a choice.

First off, the club needed to bring in more money, which meant they needed to find a way to fill seats on nights when they didn't have a big-name headliner performing. Second, Deon said that he heard Mr. Roger tell Jack, "You need to give Ms. Pat her own show," so Jack had pressure from his boss. But maybe the biggest reason I got that show was because Sheryl Underwood called Jack a dumbass in front of a bunch of other comics.

Sheryl was headlining at Morty's a few months after D. L. The two of us were talking in the greenroom. I told Sheryl that Jack wouldn't let me emcee any weekend shows.

Just then Jack walked in.

"You stupid as hell," Sheryl told him. Jack looked around like he was trying to figure out who she was talking to. "You got this gem right here," Sheryl continued, pointing to me. "And you're not even putting her onstage. She could be making you money. But you too damn stupid to see it." Jack was so embarrassed, he practically ran out of the room.

A few days later, he pulled me aside. "I'm thinking of putting up a late show on Thursday nights," he said, like this was all his idea. "Something to bring out that late-night crowd. Are you interested in hosting?"

"Okay," I answered, trying to act casual in case this was some kind of joke.

"But understand, you'd need to do everything: book the talent, get the crowd in, all of that. You think that's something you could handle?"

Jack was trying to tell me that if anything went wrong, it would be on me: if the comic I hired bombed, or the seats weren't filled, or the comic didn't show up, or the crowd's energy was off, Jack would hold it against me and throw it in my face. I could already hear his smug ass: "See? I knew you weren't ready."

After the way he'd treated me, I didn't trust Jack for shit. But this wasn't an opportunity I could turn down. I told him I'd do it.

That's how I got my own show.

The next day I got to work calling every club comic I knew—Drew Thomas from Atlanta, J. J. Williamson from Mississippi, and Tu Rae Gordon from Philly—asking them if they wanted to headline my new show, which I named "Bust a Gut."

Jack gave me a budget of seven hundred dollars to pay myself as the emcee and the talent I booked for the night. I offered comics four hundred dollars to headline. Most accepted. But the comic I wanted for my very first show refused. "I ain't doing no forty-five minutes for that type of money," he told me. He wouldn't get onstage for less than a thousand dollars. "My fee is my fee," he said. He was a real good comic. I knew the crowd would love him. Even though I didn't have money to spare, I dug into my own pocket and paid him.

Michael would have been furious if he'd known what I was up to. I could hear his voice inside my head, *Pat, your job is supposed to pay you—not the other way around*. But Michael didn't have the entrepreneurial background I did. Every drug dealer knows that if you serve a good product, customers will come back for more. I was willing to do whatever it took to make Bust a Gut a success.

To get the word out, I made hundreds of flyers and passed them out in nail salons and grocery stores, and at the Burlington Coat Factory. I slid them underneath windshield wipers of parked cars and left them at barbershops, beauty salons, and the Old Country Buffet, down by Thirty-Eighth Street. I called damn near five hundred people from Morty's phone list and offered them free tickets to my show. My first Bust a Gut was on April 3, 2008. I did so much promotion, I had a full house.

Everybody in comedy knows that audiences love when a comic jokes around with them from the stage. So before I kicked things off that night, I scanned the room to see what I was working with: I clocked a couple who looked hella awkward, like they might be on a first date; a dude wearing a Malcolm X T-shirt sitting beside a guy who looked like Donald Trump; and a drunk-ass girl in the third row who was getting on everybody's nerves. I glanced at my phone. It was ten o'clock. With my heart pounding in excitement, I got up to start the show.

"Hey y'all, I'm Ms. Pat," I said. "Welcome to Bust a Gut!" I did a few minutes of material to get the room laughing. Then, in the middle of a joke, I paused and looked down at the drunk girl who'd been talking loudly through my set.

"Baby," I said in my most buttery Atlanta drawl. The room got quiet. All eyes were on me. "If you don't shut the fuck up," I said, "I'ma stick this titty in your mouth. I will breastfeed the fuck outta you." The crowd fell out. Even the drunk girl was laughing.

Before long, Bust a Gut got a reputation as a hilarious night of comedy. I had folks lining up around the block to see my show: college kids from Purdue, white dudes in John Deere trucker hats and plaid shirts with the sleeves cut off, and Black folks dressed to the nines. Thursday nights at Morty's might have been the only place in the state where young, old, straight, gay, Democrats, and

Republicans got along. That's the beauty of comedy. A good joke is universal. Everybody laughs the same.

I don't like to hold grudges against people who did me dirty in the early days of my career. I know karma, or God, or the universe will take care of them in the end. At least, that's what happened with Jack.

One day in March 2014, I was scrolling through my phone when I got a text from Deon. He'd sent a link to a newspaper article about a bank robbery in Bloomington, Indiana. According to the report, a Black man had approached a teller and demanded money. "He never produced a weapon," the article said, but "it was implied that he had one." Beside the story was a blurry image. I knew exactly who it was.

I called Deon right away. He was laughing so much he could hardly breathe. He said as soon as he saw the picture, he called the Crime Stoppers hotline to identify the robber. Crime Stoppers told Deon that he was the twelfth person to call in with Jack's name. There wasn't even a reward. Jack had folks snitching on him for free.

The next day, the newspaper ran a follow-up: After the robber took off with the bag of money, a dye pack hidden inside the bag exploded. When the police showed up at Jack's house, this dumbass was covered in bright-blue ink. He was arrested and booked into the county jail.

Jack's stand-up was never funny to me. But Jack trying to be a criminal mastermind was the funniest shit I ever heard.

CHAPTER 12

FAMILY MATTERS

I was in Birmingham, Alabama, about to go onstage at the Stardome comedy club, when I got the call from my daddy. He was a hundred and fifty miles away, at Grady Memorial Hospital in Atlanta. "Pat, I need you to come and get me," he said. "These white folks done cut my leg off."

Daddy explained that about a month ago, he'd stepped on a piece of glass. The cut got infected, but he didn't feel anything because his diabetes made his feet go numb. By the time he got to Grady, the infection was so bad the doctors needed to amputate. "This hospital lady say they finna put me in an old folks' home," he continued, but he didn't want to go. That's why I needed to pick him up.

I hadn't talked to my daddy in years. I didn't even know he had a foot problem. Now he was missing a whole entire leg. He passed the phone to the hospital lady. "She gon' tell you everything you need to know," he said.

A woman came on the line and introduced herself as the hospital social worker. "Your father's surgery went well," she said. "But he'll require ongoing medical care." She explained that the hospital had made arrangements for him to be transferred to a rehabilitation facility. “However,” she said, pausing to clear her throat, “your father seems somewhat, uh, resistant. We’re wondering if you—or perhaps another family member—might be able to provide care in your home?”

Taking care of a one-legged senior citizen wasn’t part of my life plan. But I figured that if Daddy was reaching out to me, he probably didn’t have nobody else to call. He needed help. I had to step up.

I told the social worker that if Grady could hold Daddy for the weekend, I would be there first thing Monday morning to pick him up. Then I asked her to put my father back on the phone. “Don’t worry about nothing,” I told him. “You coming to stay with us.”

I was born at Grady. I delivered my babies there, as well. Grady doctors patched me up real good after that crackhead Theotris blew my left nipple off, and again when my baby daddy shot me in the head. Grady has one of the best trauma centers in the country. I figured they probably did excellent leg amputations, too.

When I walked into Daddy’s hospital room, I was surprised by how old he looked. He’d always been a big dude, with a loud laugh and a big belly. But lying in that hospital bed, he looked like a regular old man. I peeled back the bandage to check out the stump where his leg used to be. It was all kinds of fucked-up, with flesh coming up through the stitches. There was something sticking out that looked like it might be a bone. “Who did your operation?” I asked my father. “Freddy Krueger?”

A nurse came in to check his vitals. “Miss,” I said, pointing to my daddy’s leg, “is it supposed to look like that?” The nurse put on latex gloves and examined his stump.

“With diabetics, it can take a while to heal,” she explained. She told me I’d need to keep the wound clean and change his dressing three times a day. “There’s a pharmacy in the lobby,” she added, listing the supplies I needed to buy: "A box of four-by-four sterile gauze pads, surgical tape, antiseptic solution, hand sanitizer, blue pads, and some latex gloves."

I had six hundred dollars in cash, my pay for the weekend gig opening at the Stardome for a comic named Jazzy Jay. I couldn't spend all that money on medical supplies. It was hard enough trying to convince Michael that comedy was a real job. The last thing I needed was to return home empty-handed after three days on the road. Especially since I was also bringing home another mouth to feed.

As soon as the nurse left the room, I started flinging open drawers and cabinets. I found latex gloves, a box of wipes, a roll of gauze, and some of those blue hospital pads that I could use to protect my car seats from whatever bodily fluid might come out of an elderly amputee during a seven-hour drive back to Indiana. I shoved the supplies in my purse, along with a half-used-up roll of surgical tape I found on Daddy's breakfast tray.

I waited hours for the nurse to come back with my daddy's discharge papers. She gave me written instructions on how to clean the wound and a stack of handwritten prescriptions from the doctor. My father was on insulin for his sugar; he needed antibiotics to keep his leg from getting infected; there was a prescription for ointment to rub on the stump, pills for his high blood pressure, and other pills for the pain. "You need to get these filled right away," the nurse said before she turned and left the room.

Soon after, a man from the hospital's transport team came through to put Daddy in a wheelchair. The three of us rode down the elevator together. The transport man waited with my daddy while I went off to get the car. I pulled up to the curb, and the two of us helped Daddy into the back seat.

"Good luck," the man said, turning to go back inside the hospital.

"Hold up," I said. "You ain't leaving me the wheelchair?"

"No, ma'am."

"How I'm supposed to get him around?"

The man shrugged.

"You don't have no crutches?"

"No, ma'am."

"A cane?"

"Nah."

I couldn't believe Grady was sending me home with a post-surgery plus-size senior citizen man wearing an adult diaper and missing a leg without even a damn tree branch to help him get around.

"Gotdamn fucking piece-of-shit hospital," I muttered under my breath as I pulled away from the curb.

From Grady, I went right to CVS to drop off his prescriptions. The pharmacist said they'd be ready in forty-five minutes. So I drove to Walmart, left Daddy sitting in the back seat in the parking lot, and went inside to pick up adult diapers, a pair of men's pajama bottoms, and air freshener for the car. Before heading back to Daddy, I took out my cell phone to call Michael. I needed to let him know that I wasn't coming home alone.

Ever since we'd left the hospital, I'd kept it together. But as I dialed Michael's number, all the frustration I'd been holding back suddenly rushed to the surface.

"Hey, baby," he answered. At the sound of his voice, I burst into tears.

"These doctors are expecting Daddy to stand on one leg like a damn stop sign," I told him. "He's too damn feeble to hop. How's he supposed to get around?"

"Pat," Michael said slowly, "you bringing home your daddy, but who's taking care of him? And we only got three bedrooms. Where's he gonna sleep?"

I'd called Michael to make me feel better. But I forgot that he's not good with sudden changes. The problem with having a stable childhood, like Michael did, is you don't learn how to roll with the punches. In Michael's family, every day was pretty much the same. His mama made him hot biscuits and gravy every morning; he went to sleep in the same bed every night.

In my family, I'd wake up not knowing if I was going to get beat or fed or molested that day. At night, I didn't know if I'd have a pallet to sleep on or if I'd have to lie down on a pile of dirty-ass clothes. I learned early on how to improvise.

I wasn't expecting that call from my daddy. But when I heard his predicament, I didn't waste any time thinking about how I'd take care of a peg-leg diabetic senior citizen. Or what it would mean for Michael and the kids. I didn't consider the number of bedrooms or caregiving duties or how this new responsibility might turn our lives upside down. I just knew that once I brought him home, we'd find a way to make it work. But Michael doesn't have that chaos home training. I could tell he was getting lost in the sauce, trying to think through sleeping arrangements.

"He don't have nobody to take him in," I told Michael. "We'll figure everything out when I get home."

CHAPTER 13

DADDY'S HOME

After performing back-to-back nights in Birmingham, then dealing with the bullshit at Grady Hospital, I was wiped out, tired in that way that makes you see double. It would take seven more hours to drive back to Indiana. I needed to find a bed and lie down for a few hours before we hit the road.

My brother Andre lived in Atlanta. He was the first call I made.

"I can't do it, Pat," he said. Andre's wife was pregnant and they didn't have room for two people to spend the night.

My sister was on drugs and my other two brothers were in jail. I didn't have any other family to call, so I reached out to a friend.

Ms. Jeanne lived around the corner from us back when we were in Riverdale. My niece LaDontay and Ms. Jeanne's son ran track together. But we got close over our shared love of HGTV. The two of us gossiped about the hosts like we knew these people in real life. I was embarrassed to ask for help, but Ms. Jeanne is a real one. When I told her my situation, she didn't hesitate. She got me a hotel room for the night. "I'll pay you back," I promised.

"Don't worry about that," she said. "Just get your daddy home." I thanked her and headed back to CVS to pick up my father's medications.

The pharmacist had a round face and salt-and-pepper hair that he wore in a big old-school Afro, like Don Cornelius. With the fluorescent light shining behind him, it looked like a giant halo.

"Evening, miss," he said when I returned to his window. As I got my daddy's medications together, he asked me if my father had Medicare Part D.

"What's that?"

"Part D covers medication. It's the drug plan for seniors."

I turned to my daddy in the back seat and asked if he had it.

"I don't know what I have," he said. "But don't you worry, the Good Lord has me covered."

"He doesn't have it," I told the pharmacist.

"Ah, I see," he said. "Will you be paying out of pocket, then?"

"I guess."

He rang up the antibiotics, insulin, heart medication, painkillers, and salve to keep my daddy's open leg wound clean. Then he turned to me. "That'll be six hundred and fifty-nine dollars," he said.

For the second time that evening, I felt my eyes fill with tears. I started rambling, telling CVS Don Cornelius all my troubles. I told him we had to drive all the way back to Indiana and that my daddy's leg just got cut off and that he hadn't even been around when I was young. "I don't have enough for all that medication," I added. "Can I buy one pill of everything to get my daddy through the night?"

The pharmacist furrowed his brow and started going through the medications one by one. "You can go a day or two without these," he said, moving a bottle to the side. "And you can try Tylenol instead of this for pain," he added, moving another bottle over. "But this," he said, holding up a white box with purple writing, "is for his diabetes. This is essential. He can't go without this. And I can't fill a partial prescription. You'll need to purchase the full amount. It's three hundred and eighty-nine dollars," he said.

He must have seen the pain in my eyes, because his voice grew soft. "Wait here for a moment," he said. "Let me see what I can do."

It turned out the pharmacist used the same insulin as my daddy. That angel with an Afro filled his prescription and then gave his insulin to me.

"I want you to promise me that as soon as you get home, you'll get your daddy to a doctor and get all this straightened out," he said, handing me the medication.

"Yes, sir," I replied, thanking him for his kindness.

When I pulled out from the drive-thru, I heard Daddy in the back seat. "See, I told you," he said. "The Lord makes a way outta no way." He was right. Our Heavenly Father had just saved my daddy's ass with an angel willing to commit medical fraud. I just hope His angel didn't get caught. "God is good," Daddy said.

"All the time," I replied.

I never knew my mama and daddy as a couple. I learned the story of their relationship from my aunt Alma. I'm not sure if I believe everything she said.

According to her, the two of them met in a nightclub in Underground Atlanta sometime in the late 1960s. Aunt Alma says my mama had a "gentle nature," but I didn't see any of that when I was growing up. Maybe Mildred had been sweet and kind when she was younger. By the time I came along, she was broken, angry, and mean.

Alma said my mama would ask her to watch me when I was little. "Then she'd be gone for three, four days at a time," Alma added. "She'd be at the juke joint, drinking and selling tail. That's how Mildred was." I never saw or heard anything about my mama selling no pussy. So I don't know if Alma got her facts straight about Mildred's part-time work.

The way Alma described it, my parents had a "love-hate relationship." Meaning they loved to hate each other. She made it sound like they was always fighting and drinking and drinking and fighting and then making up and doing the whole damn thing all over again.

"One time he wanted Mildred to fix him some fish," Aunt Alma remembered. "She said no. Both of them carried switchblades and they got to fighting and slicing each other. Just bleeding all over the place." That violence is what tore that marriage apart.

One time, Daddy knocked out all of Mama's front teeth and then a couple of the side ones, too. Another time, he pushed her down a flight of steps, which sent her to Grady with a broken arm. The next day, my uncle came by and shot Daddy in his ass. That's when he ran off. Mama was twenty-two with five kids, no man, and only four teeth. I was still a baby when he left, too young to remember any of this.

For most of my childhood, my daddy was out of my life. Then, a few months after me and Michael started dating, he called me out of the blue. Mildred had died three years earlier. My daddy was the only parent I had left. He said he was calling to let me know that his mama, who lived in Alabama, was dying of cervical cancer, and did I want to meet her before she was gone? I didn't even know I had a granny.

Me and Michael left the kids with my cousin for a few days, then drove my daddy to see his kin. I met my granny, Hattie Mae, in the hospital. She was in a double room with a little old lady who looked Michael up and down before glancing in my direction. She sucked her teeth, turned back to Michael, and said, "Baby, you a fine-looking man. Sho' can do a lot better than this heifer right heah."

I busted out laughing and asked how long she'd had dementia. After that trip to Alabama, my daddy became part of my life. He didn't live too far away from our house in Riverdale. When I was working long hours, he'd come over and watch the kids. If Michael got home before me, Daddy would sit in the big green armchair waiting on me to get back. At first, Michael thought I'd asked my daddy to spy on him. But I reminded Michael that Daddy missed out on family life with his own kids. Maybe we were his chance to see that lifestyle up close. He'd sit in that green armchair for hours, just taking it all in.

I could see he enjoyed being around the children, but I sometimes got a feeling that he wasn't at ease with me. "Your mama musta told you about me . . ." he said one evening, his voice trailing off.

"All she said was, 'Your daddy ain't shit,'" I told him. But Mildred said that about everybody, including the mailman and the dude on TV who read the six o'clock news. The only man Mildred truly loved was Bob Barker, the host of *The Price Is Right*. When the theme song came on, she'd brighten like a sunflower. "Oooowee," she'd say. "Here comes my show." I think her secret fantasy was for Bob to show up one day and bless her with a Westinghouse self-cleaning oven.

"Never mind what Mama said," I told my father. "Why don't we just start fresh and get to know each other?" Giving him a chance to start over seemed to ease his mind.

We spent some good times together as a family when we was in Atlanta. After we moved to Plainfield, me and Daddy only talked once in a while by phone. Never in my wildest dreams did I think he would come crashing back into my life missing half a leg and wearing an adult diaper.

It was near midnight when I finally pulled into the hotel.

At the front desk, I got the room key and asked the man behind the counter if he could lend me an office chair with wheels. I helped my daddy out of the car and into the chair and pushed him to our room.

I got him in the shower, helped clean him up, gave him his medicine, and put him to bed. A few hours later, I woke up from a deep sleep to the sound of heavy breathing. Daddy needed to use the bathroom. He didn't want to ask for help. He was on his belly trying to pull himself across the floor.

The next morning, I helped him back into the car and we headed out for the seven-hour drive back to Indiana. I noticed he wasn't eating. I guess he thought if he didn't put anything past his lips he wouldn't need that adult diaper. His body refused to play along.

"I'm so sorry," he said, again and again, as my car filled with the smell of shit.

"It's okay, Daddy," I told him. "You gonna be all right."

I pulled over onto the shoulder of I-75, helped him lie down in the back seat, and put on a pair of latex gloves.

I used to wonder about how my life might have been different if my daddy had stuck around to raise me. His absence left a hunger that I felt all the way into my adulthood. Maybe God was trying to heal that pain. Because that afternoon on the side of the highway, me and my daddy were closer than any father and daughter could ever want to be.

It took us almost nine hours to get to Plainfield. I don't think I'd ever felt so relieved to be home. It's not easy taking care of a one-legged senior citizen with diabetes. But at least now I didn't have to do it alone. My daddy's care and upkeep became a whole-family affair.

The first time I left my father alone with Michael, he called me about an hour after I left the house. It was a Thursday night; I was at Morty's getting ready for my show. "Your daddy messed himself,"

Michael said. "I'm not no nurse, Pat. I can't change a man's Pamper." I told Michael to put Junebug on the phone. That's how my nine-year-old son learned to change adult diapers.

Junebug is the most nurturing of all my children. He loved taking care of his granddaddy. He'd clean and change the bandage on Daddy's stump every morning before school and again in the afternoon. In the evening, he'd brush his granddaddy's two teeth and give his granddaddy a bath.

Michaela wouldn't do none of that. "I'm not wiping his butt," she said. "It's unhygienic. I could get E. coli or dysentery." She held up her hand. "You know I suck my thumb." Instead, she took on all the cooking, making sure her granddaddy was well-fed. Nikia drove Daddy to his doctors' appointments. I took care of everything else.

I took him to the Social Security office to enroll him in Medicare, then to a diabetes doctor to get his insulin prescriptions. That doctor referred us to an orthopedic surgeon to see about Daddy's leg.

The leg doctor was an older white man with silver hair and an office on the hospital's first floor. When he walked into the exam room, he nodded hello to me, smiled at my daddy, then carefully unwrapped the bandage. At home, we'd been cleaning the stump and changing the bandage three times a day, like the nurse at Grady had told me. But you could tell by the stench and green pus that the wound was all infected. The bone I'd seen poking out at Grady was still sticking out from his stump.

"Okay," the doctor said as he finished his examination. "And, uh, where did you say this surgery was performed?" I could tell he was trying to be polite. What he really meant to say was, *Who the hell did this back-alley amputation? This is not how we do things around here.* The doctor scheduled my daddy for surgery so he could recut his messed-up leg and sew it back up right.

Daddy was discharged from the hospital a few days later. After that, a nurse came out to the house once a week to check his wound and make sure it was healing. They also hooked him up with an electric wheelchair and got him fitted for a brand-new fake leg.

My daddy was happy in Indiana. He joined a church, drove Junebug to tutoring, and watched his grandson play football. In Plainfield, everybody called him "Pop." His only problem was that leg.

When Daddy went to get fitted, we found out that brown-colored legs were on back order. For a few months, he had to use a Caucasian prosthetic instead. His new white leg was lightweight, with comfortable padding. The foot fit right inside his shoe. But my daddy was an old Black man from Alabama. It didn't sit well with him to have an interracial relationship in his lower half. He kept looking down, shaking his head, and muttering under his breath, "Good God Almighty, this ain't right at all."

After he'd been living with us nearly five years, my daddy started behaving strangely. A decade earlier, he'd been diagnosed with multiple myeloma. He was treated and went into remission. In Indiana, a doctor told us that the cancer had come back and had made its way to my daddy's brain.

With the cancer, he was unsteady. Sometimes he got confused. One day, when he was driving our Chevy Trailblazer, he hit the gas instead of the brake and drove right through the back wall of the garage.

He got sicker and sicker. When we thought he was running out of time, we brought him to the hospital. But my daddy told the nurses and all his church friends that he wasn't going nowhere until he saw his baby girl on TV.

A week later, I was going to be a plaintiff on the daytime court show *Judge Joe Brown*. The way my daddy was so excited, you'd think I was starring in a Netflix special.

The court case was about our house in Riverdale. When we moved to Plainfield, we'd rented it out. The lady who moved in tore the whole place up. There was dog shit everywhere. The bedroom door was busted. Our tenant refused to pay, so I took her ass to small-claims court.

I always wondered how people ended up on those daytime TV court shows. It turns out those programs have researchers who go to local courthouses and search through recently filed cases looking for something good. That's how they found me. I thought TV exposure might be good for my career. So when a producer set up a call to hear my side, I made sure to tell the story with as much charisma as I could.

"This woman had booty beads on the bathroom floor!" I said.

"*Booty beads?*" the producer asked.

"Yes, ma'am, sex toys," I explained. "I didn't know what they was, either. I got four kids and stretch marks. I don't need to decorate my behind." The producer laughed her head off. They flew me out to Los Angeles and put me on the show.

A few days before my episode of *Judge Joe Brown* was set to air, my daddy slipped into a sleep so deep I thought he might not ever wake up. But that morning, like a miracle, my daddy's eyes popped wide open. The nurse put a pillow behind his head and propped him up in his hospital bed. I stood by his side, watching him watching me complain to a TV judge that my Riverdale tenant had left booty beads on the bathroom floor. "That's my daughter right there!" my daddy said. I'd never seen him look so proud.

After the show, the nurses took him for dialysis to clean out his kidneys. He fell back into a deep sleep, so the doctors transferred him to a nursing home.

Late one night after they moved him, I found myself tossing and turning, unable to sleep. It felt like my daddy's spirit was calling out for me. I put on my clothes and went to see him. He'd been asleep for days. But as I stood by his bedside, he opened his eyes and saw me standing there. "Thank you," he whispered. I think he'd been waiting for me to get there so he could thank me before he passed on.

I rubbed his leg and told him we all loved him. "You don't need to fight no more," I whispered. "It's okay for you to go." I felt his body go cold and his spirit lift away.

My daddy died a happy man. He had a good life with us.

CHAPTER 14

GOD IS GOOD

When I was fourteen years old, I lived in a one-room efficiency in Vine City with my mama, Sweetie, and Sweetie's baby girl, LaDontay. Space was tight. Mildred slept on one sofa; me and my baby Ashley slept on another; Sweetie and her baby slept on a pallet on the floor. During the day, we shoved that pallet in the shower so we wouldn't have to walk on Sweetie's bed just to get across the room.

Since me and Sweetie was living with Mama when we had our babies, the government added the money for our children onto Mama's welfare check. But this was the middle of the 1980s, back when politicians and everybody else was complaining about "welfare queens." In their bullshit stories, poor Black women were turning themselves into baby-making machines to get that free welfare money and extra food stamps. I never met one of these "queens" in real life. Everybody I knew on public assistance stayed struggling.

To keep us from "beating" the system, the government went out of its way to make sure that assistance was always less than what a mama actually needed to survive. In Georgia, welfare checks to families with dependent children were lower than in almost every other state in the country. I guess our politicians thought the best way to crack down on these imaginary welfare queens was to make sure mamas and their babies suffered. When I had Ashley, Mama's welfare only went up by thirty-four dollars. She gave that money to me. I had to make it last an entire month.

Formula cost almost four dollars a can. Pampers cost eight dollars for a pack of thirty. But babies be eating and shitting all day long. It only took about ten days before that thirty-four dollars was gone. I wasn't even buying the good Pampers, either. I bought the off-brand diapers, where you had to put a rag inside to keep shit from exploding out the baby's ass. When those ran out and I was out of money, I'd wrap Ashley's butt in an old T-shirt and rinse it out in the sink.

When Ashley was eight weeks old, I took her to the clinic at Grady Hospital for a checkup, just like I was supposed to. A middle-aged nurse measured Ashley's head, checked her weight, then asked me how I was doing. I didn't want her looking down on me, so I lied and told her I was good. I buttoned Ashley into a striped onesie my brother stole from the Goodwill, walked out of the clinic, and got on the bus home.

I didn't notice the raggedy old man in the seat next to me until he reached out his hand and started begging for some money. "Spare a dollar, miss?" he asked. "I'm real hungry." He had sad, watery eyes, dirty fingernails, and was dressed in a sweatshirt so old I couldn't tell its original color.

I shook my head no.

"Just lemme hold a couple of quarters. I'm trying to get me something to eat."

Again, I shook my head.

I had a ten in my pocket, but that money was for formula and diapers. I didn't have a cent to spare.

"Miss," he said again.

"I don't have nothing," I said back.

That's when I heard a voice talking to me in my head. Loud and clear, the voice said, *Give that man your money*. I knew it had to be God speaking because this felt like some type of test.

Hell no, that's all I got, I told the Lord. *I need it for my baby.* I stuck my hand in the front pocket of my jeans and gripped that ten-dollar bill so tight Hamilton started hollering.

God spoke back, even louder: "Little girl, I know you're not trying to argue with me. I told you, GIVE THAT MAN YOUR MONEY."

As broke as I was, I wasn't stupid enough to play with God. I pulled my hand from my pocket and gave the dirty-sweatshirt man that crumpled-up ten-dollar bill. It felt like losing a limb.

I got off the bus, fighting back tears. My main job as a mama was to keep my baby from going hungry. Ashley wasn't even three months old and already I was fucking up. Then, out of the corner of my eye, I caught sight of something on the sidewalk that looked like a miracle. I bent down and picked up a crisp hundred-dollar bill. If I hadn't been walking with my head hanging so low, I might've missed the blessing God laid in my path. My kindness had been rewarded tenfold, just like the Bible says.

I don't think folks ought to do good deeds just to score points with the Lord. But I do think He appreciates folks who take care of His people. God blessed me when I gave my last ten to a man in need. Years later, in Plainfield, He showered me with a blessing again.

My daddy died on a Sunday afternoon. The last years of his life were spent surrounded by family who loved him. Maybe God wanted to let me know he appreciated me taking care of Daddy. Because the next day, I was surprised with one of the most exciting phone calls of my comedy career.

I was stopped at a red light at the corner of East Main and Quaker Boulevard on the way to the nursing home to pick up my father's belongings when my phone rang with a call from a number I didn't recognize.

It was my comedy agent, Carter. He'd signed me six months earlier, after seeing me open for another comic at a Laugh Out Loud in San Antonio, Texas.

"You got a minute to talk?" he asked.

"Sure," I said. "What's up?" Agents are supposed to help comics by hooking them up with opportunities, like comedy festivals, corporate gigs, or TV appearances. But Carter had never called me before. I'd thought he'd forgotten all about me.

Carter explained that his agency also represented Katt Williams and that Katt was putting together a tour. Carter had sent Katt a link to a YouTube video of me doing stand-up. "Katt thinks you're really funny," Carter said. "He wants to add you as an opener.

"The tour kicks off in Texas," Carter continued. "Then a couple of dates in Mississippi, then Virginia, Kentucky, and Missouri. You'll end in LA, where Katt's taping his special on New Year's Eve. So you'll be on the road for about two months."

I sat at the intersection with my phone pressed to my ear and my heart pounding out my chest. In all the hopes and dreams I had about comedy, I'd never imagined a chance like this. I'd gone on the road to open for club headliners before. But Katt was on a whole different level. He didn't play comedy clubs or even theaters; he sold out ten- or fifteen-thousand-seat arenas.

"You in?" the agent asked. "Because we don't have a lot of time. Things are moving fast." Carter had called me on a Monday morning.

He said if I wanted the gig, I'd need to be in Texas by Thursday afternoon.

Ever since my Thursday night show at Morty's took off, I'd been getting steady work opening for club headliners in cities around the South and Midwest.

On Fridays, after I finished working my shift at Taco Bell, I'd get in my car and drive all over the damn place—to the Laugh Factory in Chicago, Top Flite Club in Tallahassee, Improv in St. Louis, Comedy Zone in Charlotte, and Acme in Minneapolis.

DeRay Davis, one of the comics I opened for, was a real good dude. Most headliners give their openers about ten minutes of stage time, but DeRay always let me go longer. One time he said I could keep going until I ran out of material. I stayed onstage for almost forty minutes.

Another comic I opened for treated me like shit. He *never* let me go over my ten minutes. He never helped me pay for gas. One time, he had me drive nine hours to open for him at a club in Jackson, Mississippi. The club gave him three hotel rooms for the night. One room was for the headliner. The second was for his manager. The third room was supposed to be for me. But the comic gave away my room to some chick he was messing with. He knew I was dead-ass broke and he still left me without a place to stay.

Ever since we moved to Indiana, comedy had been humbling the shit outta me. I'd learned to hold my tongue when I was pissed off and not to throw hands when I was mad. I'd been paying my dues and playing the long game. But I was getting sick and tired of being patient. I was hungry for a chance to level up.

I knew that going on the road for eight weeks was the type of thing Michael would want to discuss in advance. His planning ass would want to talk logistics about this, that, and the other. But when one of the hottest comics in the game invites you out on tour, there's only one right answer.

"Hell yeah," I told Carter. "I'm in."

The next day, I had so much shit to do I was running around like a chicken with no head. I had to get my nails done and my outfits together. I had to work my shift at Taco Bell, then tell the supervisor I quit. In between all that, I also had to make the arrangements for laying my daddy to rest.

The first thing I did was call Mutual of Omaha, where Daddy had a ten-thousand-dollar life insurance policy. He'd bought the policy more than twenty years earlier. It was one of the only financially responsible things that man ever did. But when I gave the Mutual of Omaha representative my daddy's policy number, the woman on the other end of the line said, "Ma'am, I'm sorry but that account has been closed."

That made no sense. The only reason poor folks get life insurance is to make sure their family can give them a proper burial. It's not no life insurance; it's insurance to make sure you won't meet your maker in an old refrigerator box. Me and Michael needed that money to buy a casket and pay for the funeral. "That can't be right," I told the representative. I asked her to check again.

I heard the click-clack of her keyboard. "Ah, there it is," she said. I thought she'd found the money. But instead, she just gave me a date: July 22, 2011. That was the day my father had cashed out his policy. I was so mad, I wanted to bring him back to life so I could mollywhop his one-legged ass and then kill him again myself.

I couldn't believe he'd taken that money without even telling us.

I was even more mad because I had a good idea where the money had gone. I was sure my daddy got conned.

For all his faults, Daddy was a God-fearing man. He spent hours every day praying over the phone with his pastor, Apostle Odessa Lavern, back in Atlanta. When they prayed, I could hear them through his bedroom door. It was some of that Holy Roller speaking in tongues–type worship.

"She ain't got no damn Holy Spirit," I told him. "That's just some jibber jabber. Even I could do that."

"You best humble yourself when you talk about the Lord," Daddy warned me. "He ain't nothing to play about." He wasn't having no type of criticism about his telephone pastor, who also happened to be his former landlady, either. According to him, Apostle Odessa Lavern was saved and sanctified, blessed and highly favored. "Don't you put your mouth in God's business," he said. "The pastor has an anointing on her life. She been ordained to shepherd His flock."

I knew that lady was messing with his mind, but when I found out Daddy was sending his phone pastor/former landlady half his Social Security check, I realized she also had her hand deep inside his pocket.

"Ain't tithing supposed to be ten percent?" I asked him. "She got you paying interest rates and late fees like she's ordained by a collection agency."

He tried telling me the money wasn't for his phone pastor; it was for the Lord. "You can't see no harvest if you don't plant the seed," he said. "This between me and God."

I was fed up. So I started holding his Social Security check and giving him just enough cash for food, gas, and taking Junebug to Arby's. I told him it was for his own good.

But when the cancer came back, I guess my daddy got scared. With his past, he was probably worried that he'd end up in the fiery pits of deadbeat daddy hell. Maybe he thought that Mutual of Omaha money would help him pass on through the pearly gates so he could rest his soul in heaven.

I'll never know if Daddy's phone pastor was a real woman of God or a con artist who seduced him with religion. All I know is that she reminded me of the salesman at the buy-here, pay-here car lot and the shady Decision One broker. She sounded like another hustler, scamming folks with empty promises.

That's why I talk to God one-on-one, in private. When I have hopes and dreams or need some guidance, I'm not paying no ten thousand dollars to no middleman. I go directly to the source.

On Thursday morning, I flew to Texas to meet up with Katt Williams's tour. I had barely finished checking into the hotel when I got a call from Katt's road manager telling me to come to Katt's room for a kickoff meeting with the other opening acts.

This wasn't no room; it was a big-ass suite, with a separate living room that looked like a floor display at Havertys. There was a full-size cream-colored sofa with matching armchairs and beige carpet thick enough to lose a toddler in. There was a fully stocked bar, and an oval dining table with a silver bowl filled with real-looking fake lemons and limes. When I got there, Katt was finishing up a conversation in the bedroom, which was behind a set of double doors. I tried to act like this wasn't my first time in a luxury accommodation. But it was the most beautiful hotel room I'd ever seen.

While we waited on Katt to start the meeting, the other comics chopped it up in the living room. I stepped off to the side and called Michael to check on things at home. Michael said he'd called the funeral home to ask about prices. "They told me it's gonna be at least ten thousand for the burial," he said. "I don't know where we gonna get that type of money."

"You need to call the funeral director back and tell him that Daddy's missing a leg."

"Why?"

"He's only got three-quarters of a body. Maybe we can get a discount on the casket," I said. "If we cut off the other leg, they could put Daddy in a coffin for a little person and charge us half price." I thought I was speaking quietly. But my quiet voice is what most people would call loud. Katt must have overheard my conversation. After the meeting, he pulled me aside.

"It sounds like you lost a loved one," he said. When I told him my father had passed away a few days back, Katt disappeared into the bedroom. He returned holding four stacks of hundred-dollar bills, each worth a thousand dollars. He pressed the money into my hand. "Go bury your daddy," he said.

Before Katt, I thought celebrities only gave money to people in need because they wanted the good publicity. But when Katt slid me that cash, it was quiet and discreet. He didn't do it for clout. He gave from his heart.

That four grand helped pay for the funeral and gas money I gave my brother Andre so he could drive himself and our sister up from Atlanta to attend the service. We buried our daddy on a Wednesday. The next day, Katt flew me back out to catch up with the tour in Mississippi. I didn't miss a single show.

Katt didn't only help me with my daddy's funeral costs. He was a generous dude all the way around. He'd booked five openers for his tour. After every show, he paid us in cash an amount that was almost eight times what I made opening for club comics for an entire weekend. And usually when a big comic is on the road, he'll stay in the best hotel in each city and put his opener someplace cheaper. Katt didn't do that. If he was staying at the Ritz-Carlton, then we *all* got to stay at the Ritz-Carlton. That's how I discovered that I love a good 400-thread-count Egyptian cotton bedsheet and extra-plush towels in the bathroom. I was tempted to put some of that fancy hotel shit in my suitcase and bring it home to Michael, but I was too scared I'd get caught.

As long as I'd been in comedy, I'd never seen this type of lifestyle before. I loved the amenities—the hotel lobbies that smelled like flowers and the little chocolates housekeeping left on my pillow at night. But I never let it go to my head. I kept reminding myself, *This ain't your real life.* When the tour was over, I'd be right back in the comedy trenches, driving all over the damn place opening for club headliners, getting paid six or seven hundred dollars for an entire weekend.

Still, I had a feeling that I'd been put on Katt's tour for a reason. My spirit told me this was a message from God. He was letting me know that something better was out there for me. This was my reminder to keep grinding and never give up.

CHAPTER 15

MICHAEL ON BOARD

Katt Williams is a family man. He has ten children, seven of them adopted. He brought all those kids, their nannies, and his dogs with him out on tour. He likes to keep his loved ones close. That's probably why he asked me about Michael one night in Norfolk, Virginia, after our show at the Chartway Arena.

Katt had invited everyone back to his hotel suite to hang out. I was sitting on the sofa, talking shit and cracking jokes, when out of nowhere, Katt turned to me and asked, "What does your husband think of you doing comedy?"

The question caught me off guard. I didn't know how to answer. The truth was, I'd been doing comedy for almost a decade and not once had Michael ever come to see me perform.

When I was doing open mics in Atlanta, Michael stayed home to watch the kids. After we moved to Indiana, he didn't come to my Thursday night shows at Morty's because he had to get up for work early Friday morning. But even on the weekends, or when he had time off from work, or after the kids got old enough to stay home alone, he *still* didn't come to my shows.

Michael never came right out and said so, but I knew deep down he didn't support my comedy because to him, unless you were Eddie Murphy or Jerry Seinfeld famous, telling jokes wasn't a real career.

Michael came from a long line of hardworking union men. To him, a job meant regular hours, good benefits, and a steady paycheck. You get none of that in comedy. The hours were horrible. The pay was even worse.

Back when we were in Riverdale, a comic asked me to open for him at a club in Hinesville, Georgia. It was the first time I ever got paid to do stand-up. That night, I made fifty dollars. When Michael found out, he couldn't believe it. "That's a three-and-a-half-hour drive," he said. "Fifty dollars don't even cover the cost of gas. They taking advantage of you, Pat," he added. "This is worker exploitation."

He didn't understand that it's just how comedy works. In the beginning, a new comic is expected to do low-paying club gigs because that's how you get better. And I wanted to get better because I loved comedy. I loved being onstage and hearing that laughter. I loved having all those eyes on me. When I was little, I was invisible. Nobody listened to what I had to say or cared about what I did. With comedy, I felt seen and heard.

Plus, I was good at it. I knew if I worked hard enough, put in the stage time, made the right connections, wrote enough jokes, and worked on my material until I had a tight forty-five-minute set, it would pay off in the end. But it's a process. Like every other comic, I had to pay my dues.

You'd think a man who laughed his balls off watching *Seinfeld* would be at least a little interested in the comedy scene. But Michael couldn't care less. In fact, the longer I worked at getting my career off the ground, the more irritated he seemed to get.

Michael is very protective. When I started going out on the road, he worried that it wasn't safe for me to be driving alone late at night in cities I didn't know. When I told him I was working on material about being a drug dealer, he worried that if I put my business in the street, people would use it against me. When I got my Thursday night show at Morty's, he complained that I stank of cigarette smoke when I came home and got into bed. It seemed like he had a problem with everything comedy related.

I thought maybe I could win him over by earning more money. So I started selling merch to supplement the pay I made as an opener doing weekend gigs on the road. My bestseller was a hand towel I printed with the words IF YOU WANT IT, I'LL WASH IT, the punch line to a joke I made about foreplay with my husband. On a good weekend, I might make an extra five hundred dollars just from sales, which meant I'd bring home more than a thousand. But with gas, food, and unexpected expenses, sometimes I came home with a whole lot less.

One time, me and Michael really got into it about the hours I was keeping, the miles I was putting on the car, and the time I was spending away from the kids. "And for what?" Michael asked. "To make a few hundred dollars? It don't make financial sense."

I reminded him about all the money we spent the year he decided to join a softball team. "I bought you a three-hundred-dollar baseball bat and a leather glove," I said. "Then I sat on the bleachers in the blazing sun, and you ain't got not a single run. The only time you got to first base was when the pitcher hit you with the ball. You were the worst player in the whole league," I added. "But I never told you to quit."

Michael tried to tell me that playing ball and doing comedy are not the same thing. "That was a mandatory after-work activity," he insisted. "My boss asked me to play. It's not like I could tell him no."

"Well, I love this comedy shit," I told him. "I know it's going to turn into something big. I can *feel* it. So I'm not gonna stop."

After that argument, the two of us got locked into a don't-ask, don't-tell standoff. He didn't ask me to quit comedy. And I didn't tell him to come to any of my shows. That's how we kept the peace.

When Katt asked me what my husband thought of my stand-up, I didn't get into the whole backstory. I just told him, "Michael's never seen me perform."

"For real?" Katt exclaimed. "Man, that's crazy." He asked me to get Michael on the phone so he could personally invite him to our next show. We were playing at the KFC Yum! Center in Louisville, Kentucky, about a two-hour drive from Plainfield. Katt told Michael to bring the kids. "Your wife's real funny," he said. "I know you're gonna dig the show."

Every audience has its own special energy. You have warm rooms and cold rooms, good audiences and bad. When the room is cold, the crowd will stare back at you, blank-faced, waiting for you to prove that you're funny. It's like they want you to drag the laughs out of them. But when the room is good and toasty, it feels like the crowd is starving for laughs and all you need to do is feed them. I'd been doing comedy clubs long enough that I could feel if a room was hot or cold even before I got onstage.

But playing an arena is a whole different thing. With the stage lights, I couldn't see people's faces or read their body language. I didn't know if folks were smiling or looking bored. Instead, I had to go by vibes. If the crowd was enjoying my set, the energy would roll in like a tidal wave; when a joke hit, the sound of laughter felt like thunder.

The night we performed at the KFC Yum! Center in Louisville, I was so nervous my stomach was in knots. I prayed for a good crowd and tried not to think about Michael, Nikia, Junebug, and Michaela, who were sitting to my left, in section 104, row DD.

Comedy is a lot like sex—once you get a good rhythm going, it just gets better and better. That night me and that crowd was slammin'. They hit me with that good, good energy, and I hit them right back with funny-ass jokes. The first time Michael ever saw my comedy, I was in front of ten thousand people having one of the best sets of my life.

After the show, my family came backstage to meet Katt. I pulled Nikia aside and asked him how I did. He said that when I was onstage, he'd looked over at his daddy and saw Michael with his head in his hands, slumped down in the chair. "He was worried you was gonna bomb," Nikia said. "But then everybody started laughing. We told him you did really good."

Nikia said he really liked the show. Junebug gave me a big hug. Michaela, the smart-ass of the family, smiled and said I was "surprisingly not bad." But Michael was quiet. I didn't get a "Good job," or "I'm proud of you," or "Baby, you did your thing." That man did not have a single nice thing to say. The only comment he had was to criticize a joke I made about the way his big toe swelled up when he had a case of gout. "It's actually a very painful condition," he said. "So I guess the joke wasn't that funny to me."

For some comics, that type of fucked-up feedback would be grounds for divorce. But my feelings don't get hurt that easy and I know my husband. Michael doesn't show his support with words. He loves me with his actions. After he saw me perform in Kentucky, Michael didn't give me compliments. Instead, he tried to help me out.

After that show, anytime I called home from the road, Michael would tell me all the funny things I had missed while I was gone. He'd describe arguments the kids had with each other, repeating the exact words this or that kid had said. One time, when he was reporting on the day's events, he said, "Hang on, I wrote it down. Lemme go find the paper." This man had been taking notes like he was on assignment for *The New York Times*. At first I didn't know what he was up to. Then suddenly, I got it. When Michael started telling me funny family stories, it was his way of saying, "Here's some material. Maybe you can use it in your act."

After years of doubt, Michael was finally invested. He saw my potential. He wanted to help me succeed. I thought he loved me when he made me an authorized user on his credit card. But when my husband started believing in my comedy dream, it felt like the greatest love of all.

CHAPTER 16

DIAMOND

Michael likes to say I have a hard shell on the outside, but inside I'm soft as a marshmallow. He thinks that's why I keep bringing home family members to live with us whenever they're in crisis. Michael came from a middle-class life, so he doesn't understand that this has nothing to do with softness—it's just broke folks' rules for family survival.

In every poor family, there's always one person who's doing better than everybody else. Maybe it's the one child who finished high school and got a good job. Or that uncle who stays out of jail. Or the cousin who married rich and has a little spending money. That person always ends up as the emergency contact for the whole damn family. In my family, that person is me.

When I was sixteen, I took in my thirteen-year-old cousin Tata. Her mama had eight kids and four grandkids in the house. The place was a hellhole. Tata needed to be out. So she came to live with me. A few weeks later, I took in my baby daddy's sister's three kids, too. Little Cee, CeCe, and Timeeka were nine, ten, and eleven. They needed a rescue after their mama, Darleene, fell in love with crack. I bought bunk beds and put all four girls in Ashley's bedroom. I drove them to school in the mornings and made sure they were fed and clean. The girls stayed with me until I got busted for selling dope and ended up in jail.

A few years later, not long after I started dating Michael, I took in Sweetie's four girls—LaDontay, Diamond, Destiny, and the baby, Jonelle—to keep them out of the system. They stayed with us for almost a decade. Next came my peg-leg diabetic daddy. Then, in 2013, a year after I finished the tour with Katt Williams, I got another call for help.

It was December, and I was fixing Christmas dinner at my cousin Boo's house in Atlanta when my niece LaDontay called. Her sister Diamond was in trouble. I hadn't seen that girl in years.

After Sweetie took her daughters away from me and Michael, I tried to stay in touch. I brought groceries over. I took the girls to the beauty shop to get their hair washed and braided. But just like I'd predicted, once they left our house in Riverdale, my nieces' lives took a turn for the worse.

Sweetie was still hittin' the pipe. She let her girls run wild. Jonelle, the youngest, got pregnant at thirteen and had six children by the time she was twenty-one. She got caught up in a home invasion gone bad and landed in prison on a twenty-five-year bid. Destiny's baby got taken away after Destiny burned the baby's foot trying to give him a bath while she was high. Diamond had her first baby, a boy, at seventeen. She named her son Jamal. She went on to have three more babies she couldn't take care of. Just like my sister, Diamond got hooked on drugs.

In the end, only my oldest niece, LaDontay, who was halfway through her senior year when she left us, graduated high school, stayed off drugs, and got herself a full-time job.

After we moved to Plainfield, I'd check up on the girls on

Facebook. LaDontay posted pictures of her beautiful family. Meanwhile, Diamond would be acting a fool, smoking, drinking, and getting high, just like her mama. After a while, she stopped posting. For years, I thought she was lost to the wind. But when LaDontay called that Christmas, she knew where Diamond was.

My niece was staying over by her baby daddy's cousin's house. But her baby daddy had got locked up. Now the baby daddy's cousin's family wanted Diamond out. LaDontay gave me an address. Before we headed back to Plainfield, me and Nikia drove to a run-down street in Decatur, around the corner from hell.

We found Diamond standing in the middle of a filthy living room, looking dazed, with three small children hiding behind her legs. The kids were dressed in grimy outfits that didn't make no sense. Diamond's four-year-old daughter, Tay-Tay, had on a badly stained Disney princess T-shirt with boys' pants that looked four sizes too small. Her boy Jamal was wearing winter boots, a thin blue windbreaker, underpants, and nothing else. The two-year-old, D'Sani, wore a sagging diaper and too-big tennis shoes with no laces. The room smelled like that Pamper hadn't been changed in days. The last time I'd seen children in such a pitiful situation was when I picked up Diamond and her three sisters at her mother's place, almost twenty years before.

Diamond had a fourth child: a two-week-old baby girl named Shirlene. The baby was still wrapped in her flannel hospital blanket. Diamond clutched Shirlene to her chest and asked me why I was there.

"I just came to check on you," I told her.

She said she was good, just waiting on her baby daddy. "He be out any day now," she insisted.

"Girl, that nigga ain't *never* getting out," Diamond's baby daddy's cousin blurted out from across the room. It took me damn near half an hour to convince Diamond to leave that house of horrors. "I have room," I kept telling her. "Y'all can stay with me until you get back on your feet."

She threw all her possessions into trash bags. Nikia put them in the trunk. When Diamond and her four kids climbed into the back seat, the car filled with the stank of baby shit, stale Backwoods, and body funk. It was so bad I made Nikia pull up to a gas station. I bought fifteen Christmas tree air fresheners and hung them off the rearview mirror. Then the car smelled like baby shit, body funk, stale weed, and Royal Pine.

We drove back to my cousin Boo's place. I put all those children in the bath and sent Junebug out to Walmart for diapers in size large for the toddler and extra small for the newborn. I scrubbed those children until they couldn't get no cleaner. Then we all headed back to Plainfield. Me and Michael drove Diamond and her kids in the Trailblazer. Nikia took Junebug and Michaela in his Maxima.

We were about thirty minutes outside Atlanta when I told Michael to pull over and call 911.

"What's wrong?" he asked.

I clutched my chest and gasped for breath. "I'm having a heart attack," I told him. "I need an ambulance, right now."

Michael took my hand in his. He told me to take long, slow breaths. "I think this is a panic attack," he said calmly.

"I'm panicked because I'm *dying*," I said. "I need help. *I can't breathe*."

I'd never had a panic attack before. That shit scared the hell outta me. Michael said it made sense, though: "We bringing home five more mouths to feed," he said. "We don't know how we're going to take care of them. That's a panicky situation."

He was right. I didn't have a plan. I'd jumped without thinking because when I saw those little kids—scared and hungry with no one taking care of them—it reminded me of how I used to pray for someone to come along and save me back when I was living with Mildred.

As much as Michael doesn't like sudden change, he really came through for me that night. When I was panicking, he held my hand and told me everything was gonna be all right.

I don't know exactly how Diamond was living back in Atlanta, but every part of her body, from tip to toe, was either tore up or broke down.

In Plainfield, I took her to the dentist, where she got eight rotten teeth pulled and seven fillings. I took her to the eye doctor and got her glasses so she could see. I took her to the hair spot and paid for a relaxer and sew-in.

At home, me and Michael tried to show her life skills. Like, cereal is not dinner, you gotta brush your teeth at least twice a day, and it's a mama's responsibility to teach her children how to spell their own damn names. Diamond was twenty-four years old, but she acted like this was brand-new information to her.

Getting Diamond's life together was one thing to solve. We also had to take care of all her children. The clothes Diamond packed in the trash bags were filthy, so I threw them all away. At Walmart, I bought diapers, onesies, and formula for the baby, and socks, underwear, jeans, and T-shirts for the older kids. Diamond didn't know the size of none of the children's feet, so I had to bring all of them with me to Payless.

In the store, Tay-Tay and D'Sani clung to Jamal like they was in a hurricane, and he was the only thing keeping them from blowing away. They all looked scared to death. I wondered if any of them had ever been shoe shopping before.

The lady at the Payless register must have sensed something was going on with these babies, because when I took out my wallet to pay for the shoes, she whispered that she was giving me the employee discount, 30 percent off.

Not one of Diamond's children had ever been to a doctor. They'd never been to school. The two younger girls were still in Pampers. Six-year-old Jamal didn't know his ABCs from Adam. Even though I kept telling the kids they were safe, at home they all acted like they was traumatized. Tay-Tay sucked on her fingers. D'Sani stayed wetting the bed. When they'd been with us almost six months, I discovered Jamal was hiding food.

I was looking under his bed for a missing tennis shoe when I found three bags of potato chips, a half-eaten box of cookies, two packages of ramen noodles, and three uncooked hot dogs wrapped in a paper towel. That boy had a corn dog under his pillow. When I asked him what the food was for, his lip started trembling and his eyes filled with tears. He told me the food was in case any of them got hungry. He looked terrified, like he thought I was about to tear his ass up. "I'm not mad at you," I said.

I took him to the kitchen and opened the fridge. "In this house, you can eat anytime you want," I told him. Still, it took months before that child stopped hoarding food, acting like he was one meal away from starvation. It took even longer for Michael to teach Jamal how to read.

I found the two of them sitting at the kitchen table one Sunday afternoon, staring at an easy-reader phonics book Michael had ordered online. "You can do it," Michael said, pointing to the page. Jamal looked up at him, like he wasn't sure.

"Just try," Michael coaxed.

"Tttt . . . rrrr . . . uhh . . . ck," Jamal stammered.

"Now put it all together."

"Truck!" Jamal exclaimed. "Truck. It says 'truck,' right?"

"That's right," Michael said. "You got it. Good job. That's a five-letter word. You're picking this up real quick."

Jamal shot me a big happy grin. It was beautiful to see that little boy looking so proud of himself.

Me and Michael made sure the children were well taken care of. But I knew from experience that what they needed most of all was for their mama to get her shit together.

Diamond promised that she was ready to turn her life around. "If you're ready," I told her. "I got you." I helped her enroll in a GED program. Nikia and his wife, Kiki, hooked her up with a job working the overnight shift at a wholesale bakery across town. Diamond told Kiki that she was trying her hardest to make me proud. But sometimes I'd catch her staring off in the distance. She looked so gloomy, like I'd taken her to the most miserable place on earth.

"I didn't like it here, either," I told her. "But this is a good place for your kids."

A few months after she moved in with us, Michael taught Diamond to drive. Then the bakery promoted her to shift manager, and she started making twenty dollars an hour. By the end of her first year in Indiana, my niece was doing so good that she moved into her own apartment and got herself a 2011 burgundy Impala. Michael cosigned her car lease. We were so happy to see her shine.

One night Kiki took Diamond to go see Kevin Hart at the Fieldhouse arena in Indianapolis. I bought her a cute outfit—black skinny jeans with a matching jacket and a deep purple top—and helped her do her makeup. Before the girls left, I caught Diamond checking herself out in the mirror, turning this way and that. I could see the light had come back to her eyes and hope had returned to her spirit. She was smiling at her reflection, holding her head high.

"Girl, you lookin' good," I told her. "It's nice to see you smile." Diamond had put her street days behind her. My niece had turned her life around.

During the week, Diamond worked overnight shifts, so the kids stayed with me and Michael. On the weekends, they stayed by they mama. Then one day Jamal told me that it was hard for them over there. He said his mama put the food in the top cupboard where they couldn't reach, and sometimes they went hungry. That should have been my first clue that something wasn't right.

Then there was the way Diamond was always sniffling. She said she was "sick," or it was "allergies," but Michael had his suspicions. "Her nose shouldn't be running all the time like that," he said to me. "You think she's back on drugs?"

"No," I said. "She ain't that stupid."

Then she crashed her car and started losing weight. Still, I couldn't see that she was in trouble. I didn't want it to be true.

One Tuesday afternoon, I was sitting at the kitchen table cold-calling Morty's customers, giving away free tickets for my Thursday night show. Just as I finished a call, my phone began to ring. It was a caseworker from Child Protective Services letting me know that Jamal, D'Sani, and Tay-Tay had been picked up by the police walking barefoot by themselves out in the freezing cold. At the apartment, the cops had found Diamond passed out on the sofa. When I went over to check on her, the building manager told me Diamond hadn't paid her rent in months.

"I lost my job," she told me. "I'm sorry, I fucked up." She was so ashamed, she couldn't even look me in the eye.

Diamond asked me and Michael if we could take her kids for a little while so she could focus on getting her shit together. She promised she'd do better. She kept telling me she was trying to get back on her feet.

A few weeks later, when I couldn't reach her by phone, I drove back to Diamond's apartment. The front door was unlocked, and the place was empty. All the furniture me and Michael had bought her—the bedroom set, the kitchen table, even the brand-new washer and dryer—gone. I'd seen this before. Back when I was selling crack, my customers would sell all their possessions chasing that high. As much as I didn't want to believe it, once I saw that empty apartment, I knew for sure that Diamond was back on drugs.

I walked through the apartment noticing all the familiar signs: the overflowing ashtrays, filthy toilet and bathroom sink, the kitchen cupboards without a stick of food. On the counter, Diamond had placed her children's Social Security cards lined up in a row. That's how I learned that my niece had up and left Indiana. She didn't even say goodbye.

I never asked Diamond about what her life was like after she left our home in Riverdale and went to stay by her mama. I don't know what type of trouble she got into or who did what to her. She was in middle school when my sister took her back. Anything can happen to a young girl like that when nobody is keeping her safe.

My mama tried to drown her sadness in a bottle of Bumpy Face gin. My sister turned to crack. I don't know what drugs Diamond got into. But if she's anything like her mama and her mama's mama, once that demon got her it would be damn near impossible for her to shake it loose. If Sweetie hadn't taken Diamond away from me and Michael, my niece would have had a chance at life. Me and Michael would have kept her in school and away from boys and drugs.

When Sweetie showed up to our house in Riverdale with the police and a court order, me and Michael had no choice but to give her children back. We weren't going to let that happen again. After Diamond ran off, we went down to the courthouse, filled out the paperwork, and got full custody of all four children so that nobody could take those babies away.

More than a decade has passed since Diamond left us. Her first-born, Jamal, is now a well-mannered high school senior. He loves doing renovations with Michael and wants to work in construction when he graduates. D'Sani is thoughtful, quiet, and smart as a whip. In a few years, she'll be off to college. Tay-Tay says she wants to become a radiologist. That girl loves to be up in everybody's damn business. Of course she wants to see inside their bodies, too.

Shirlene was only two weeks old and wrapped in a dirty hospital blanket when we got her from that hellhole. The only life Shirlene has ever known is here at home with us. She's the giggliest, most sunshiny, happy seventh grader you'd ever want to meet.

We couldn't save their mother. But me and Michael tried to do right by all those kids.

CHAPTER 17

WHITE BOYS

In one of my oldest memories, I'm sitting on my granddaddy's knee watching the little black-and-white TV he kept in the front room of his illegal liquor house, in Decatur, Georgia. From the outside, it looked like a regular run-down home, with bedsheets hanging in the windows and a busted screen on the front door. But inside, Granddaddy had built a plywood bar in the living room. He sold bootleg corn liquor to neighborhood drunks for fifty cents a shot. When I was little, my granddaddy was my favorite person in the world.

Every evening, I'd tuck myself under his arm and keep him company while he served his customers and talked back to whatever was happening on TV. We watched all kinds of shows together: *Good Times*, *The Jeffersons*, *Georgia Championship Wrestling*. At eleven o'clock, he tuned in to *The Tonight Show Starring Johnny Carson*.

I remember one night when we was watching, two of Johnny's guests got into it, arguing about poor folks. An older white lady wearing a long white dress that looked like a tablecloth layered over a bedsheet said that she'd grown up poor but that those types of problems didn't exist anymore in America. "Nobody dies of starvation here," she said. "You can always get some food. We have it."

The other guest, a Black man with a low Afro and a big mustache, said folks die of starvation in this country all the time. "I know we *have* food," he said. "But we don't always give it." The audience broke into applause. That guest was Richard Pryor.

"This nigga right here," my granddaddy said, slapping the bar top and beaming with pride, "he ain't told not one lie yet."

I don't think my granddaddy ever saw a Pryor movie. And he sure never saw him perform stand-up. But just like tens of millions of people around the country that night, he was glued to his set, watching Pryor tell a white lady that she was full of shit.

Back then, there was no Netflix, YouTube, or HBO. Everybody and they mama watched the same TV shows. Late night, that meant Johnny Carson. His show was so popular that he could make regular people famous overnight. He did this all the time with comedians. Jerry Seinfeld, Joan Rivers, and Roseanne Barr were unknown club comics before Carson put them on his stage. Five minutes of stand-up on *The Tonight Show* is how Roseanne got her own TV sitcom. In those days, a good set on late-night TV could turn a club comic into a star. When I became a stand-up, I wanted something like that to happen for me.

In Plainfield, I was trying hard to level up my comedy career. I saw big things in my future: theater dates, Netflix specials, a sitcom, starring me. I knew that if I kept grinding, eventually I'd make it. But I wanted to speed things up. I needed Johnny Carson–level exposure.

I knew only one place where comics could get introduced to millions of people at once: *The Bob and Tom Show.* Taped in Indianapolis, the radio program aired all over the country and was one of the most popular morning shows in the Midwest. It was like white folks' *Breakfast Club*. That's how big it was.

From 6 to 10 a.m., Bob and Tom gave their listeners news and sports, but the real highlight of the show was the stand-up comics they featured as guests. If a comic was extra funny, Bob and Tom might keep them on the air for hours, talking shit and cracking jokes. It wasn't just regular people listening, either. Comedy club bookers, agents, and other industry folks also tuned in. Just like with Carson, doors would open for comics who killed on *The Bob and Tom Show*. It was some of the best free publicity a stand-up comedian could get.

The only person I knew with the radio connections was Morty's manager, Jack. When headliners came to town to perform at Morty's, Jack would get them on *The Bob and Tom Show* to do promotion. Jack knew the booker. All he had to do was make a call and recommend me. But when I asked him to hook me up with a radio spot so I could promote my Thursday night show, he just rolled his eyes.

"You're not ready," he said.

"What you mean?"

"You're just not right for radio."

"Why not?"

"Because I said so."

"When do you think I'll be ready?"

"No time soon."

Jack wasn't going to do shit to help me. I had to find another way.

The problem with stand-up comedians is that most of them aren't morning people. So when Jack booked a comic to be a guest on *The Bob and Tom Show*, someone from the club, usually Jack or Avery, would have to wake up at the crack of dawn, pick up the comic at their hotel, and drive them to the radio station so they'd be there by seven thirty.

I knew Jack hated to get up early, so I offered to drive the headliners myself. "I got kids," I told him, "I'm already awake. It ain't nothing for me." Driving comics to the radio station was how I planned to get on air.

I figured if I stayed close to the action, sooner or later, I'd connect with somebody who could help get me on the show. For almost a year, I picked up comics, drove them to the radio station, waited in the lobby while they did the show, and then brought them back to the hotel. Jack never offered to pay me. But I kept showing up, working for free, waiting for something to happen.

One Friday morning, I was sent to pick up Ralph Harris, a Philly comic, and take him to the station. I liked Ralph. He was cool. He'd seen me perform at Morty's before. He said he thought I was funny. I also happened to know that Ralph was personal friends with Bob (or maybe Tom, I couldn't remember). When I drove him to the radio station the last time he was in town, he mentioned that he and Bob (or maybe it was Tom) had gone fishing together.

I arrived at Ralph's hotel to pick him up promptly at 6:45 a.m. He got in the car and flashed me a smile. "Hey, Ms. Pat, how you doing?"

On the drive to the station, the two of us chopped it up, talking about comics we knew and the football game coming up that weekend. We were almost at our destination when Ralph asked me if I'd ever been a guest on *The Bob and Tom Show*. This was the chance I'd been waiting for.

"No," I said. "But I really want to get on the show. You think maybe you could vouch for me?"

"Sure," he said with a shrug. "No problem." That morning Ralph introduced me to the show's booker. A week later, I was sitting in the radio booth across from Bob and Tom.

As a comic, I'm real comfortable talking to a room full of strangers. I figured talking to a couple of dudes in a radio booth wouldn't be a big deal. Then, minutes before we were going live to millions of listeners, I was hit by the worst case of nerves I've ever had. I was so damn shaky, I thought I might pass out. This was my mama's fault.

When I was little, Mildred used to warn me about talking to white folks. "Don't look them in the eye," she said. "They better and smarter than you." I don't know why she was giving me advice from the Ku Klux Klan handbook. But I was so young, I believed her. After all, the only white folks I knew back then were policemen, caseworkers, politicians, and Bob Barker from *The Price Is Right*.

It wasn't until I started doing comedy in Indianapolis that I finally started mixing and mingling with regular white folks. Hearing all those thirty-seven-year-old white-boy comics talking about how they can't get laid and their favorite person is a cat was eye-opening. I realized that Mildred had been wrong all along. There was no way in hell these dudes were smarter and better than me. Cat comedy cured my internalized racism.

I thought I'd left all those nervous feelings about white people behind me. But sitting across from Bob and Tom, the whitest white men in all the land, it all came rushing back. *They better than you. . . . They better than you. . . . They better than you. . . .* No matter how much I tried to silence them, my mama's words kept playing in my head.

I was so nervous, I felt sick to my stomach. Then suddenly, we were on air.

Bob introduced me to the audience, then asked, "So, Ms. Pat, I hear your husband has a problem with gout."

I'd listened to enough Bob and Tom to know that when they ask a guest a question like that, they're just teeing up a bit the comic has in his or her stand-up routine. That way, they're guaranteed to get a funny story because the comic has already worked it out onstage.

Experienced comedians know how to adapt material from their routine and make it work for the radio. They can add or subtract details on the fly, speed up their delivery, or pause in different places. I didn't know how to do any of that. Plus, I was hella nervous. So I just told the story about Michael's gout exactly like I do onstage. I even kept the pause after the punch line for laughter from the crowd. This is *not* how you tell a story on the radio. I'd spent almost a year networking my way into this opportunity, but I could tell I was flopping, hard.

When we cut for a commercial break, I looked down at my phone. My friend Deon had texted me. "WTF," he wrote. Deon never got up this early. He was only awake to listen to me. He texted again. "You're bombing."

"What do I do?" I texted back.

"They want a good story," he messaged. "Talk about selling crack, going to jail, whatever." Then in all caps he added: "TELL THEM YOU GOT SHOT IN THE TITTY."

I didn't think *Bob and Tom* listeners would want to hear about my areola while they drank their morning coffee. But I didn't have time to think of another story. So, while we were still on commercial break, I turned to Kristi, the news lady, who was sitting beside me, and told her about the time my crackhead customer Theotris came running down the street with a pistol and blew my left nipple right off. "I also got shot in the head," I added.

Kristi put up her hands. "Whoa, whoa, whoa," she said. "Let's save this story for on air."

I don't know how Deon knew that middle-aged white men would love a blown-off nipple story, but "TELL THEM YOU GOT SHOT IN THE TITTY" was some of the best career advice I've ever got.

Bob and Tom loved my stories of inner-city gun violence. They asked a ton of follow-up questions and laughed their asses off at every detail I shared. They kept me on the show for an entire hour.

After that appearance, they invited me back almost every month. Just like I hoped, people outside Indianapolis started learning my name, including other comics.

One afternoon, I got a call from Eddie Ifft, a comedian from LA. "I heard you're fucking hysterical," Eddie said. He told me he had a podcast called *Talkin' Shit* and invited me out to Cali to be a guest.

This was back in 2013. I didn't know what the hell a podcast was. The next day, I asked Michael.

"It's usually just folks having a conversation," he explained.

"And people listen to that?"

"A lot of people," Michael said.

Podcasts don't pay their guests, I discovered. They don't even cover travel expenses or accommodations. If I wanted to do Eddie's show, I'd have to pay for a flight, get a rental car, and book myself a hotel. The whole trip would cost at least a thousand dollars. Michael didn't think it made good business sense. Even my manager, John, thought it was a waste of money. But I had a feeling that the trip would lead to something good. When my instinct tells me to do something, I always listen.

A week later, I was sitting on a sofa in Eddie Ifft's podcast studio, which was really just his living room. I thought our conversation would sound pretty much like it did on *Bob and Tom*. What I didn't realize is that radio is controlled by the FCC, which means that if someone cusses or talks about dicks and pussy on air, the station can get fined ten thousand dollars or more. I had to keep it clean on *Bob and Tom*. But podcasts don't have those types of rules and regulations. On Eddie Ifft's show, I discovered, any-fucking-thing goes.

I barely had my headphones on before the two of us was cussing up a storm. We riffed about Eddie using the N-word, white girls getting kidnapped, and the time I ironed my panties and accidentally burned out the crotch. "You're the best guest we've ever had," Eddie said, laughing his ass off. He told his listeners to follow me on social media and called me "a one-nipple train of comedy."

Eddie's podcast kicked off the single most unexpected phase of my entire career. I was suddenly flooded with invitations from white-boy comics who wanted me on their podcasts, too. I don't know why they all wanted to speak to a middle-aged Black woman from Atlanta with six kids in the house and only one nipple, but they was passing me around like a hooker with a friends-and-family discount. I talked to Marc Maron, Bert Kreischer, Tom Segura, Joe Rogan, and Neal Brennan. One dude, Ari Shaffir, interviewed me on a park bench in Brooklyn. We talked for almost three hours. He wanted to hear everything about my life.

Ari was a tall, skinny, half-balding Jewish dude. I figured his listeners probably looked just like him. But later that week, I performed a fifteen-minute set at a comedy show in the basement of a Brooklyn bar. After the show, two Black women approached me.

One said, "I heard you on Ari Shaffir's podcast."

The other woman said, "You should write a book."

"I'd love to," I replied. "But I don't know nothing about writing."

The second woman pointed to the first. "You should ask her," she said. "She's a writer."

God sure does work in mysterious ways. I'd bought a plane ticket with Michael's credit card that led me to a bunch of white men podcasters, who led me to a Black woman journalist who helped me write my first book. And that book, *Rabbit*, would get nominated for an NAACP award in outstanding literature. I'd had a feeling that spending a thousand dollars to fly out to Cali to be on a podcast would pay off. But I couldn't ever have imagined this.

I wasn't much of a reader before *Rabbit* was published, so I didn't realize that when book readers like something, they tell all their friends. People started hitting me up on social media, saying they were reading *Rabbit* with their book clubs, or that they bought copies for their mama, their sisters, or all their aunts. One teenager said she wrote about *Rabbit* for her college essay.

After years of hoping my career would take off, I felt like things were finally happening.

Then Hollywood started to call.

CHAPTER 18

HOLLYWOOD HUSTLE

Lee Daniels's trailer on the set of *Empire*, at the Cinespace Studios lot in Chicago, was a lot bigger than it looked from the outside. It was set up like a living room, with two narrow sofas against the walls and a small coffee table in the middle. I stepped inside, introduced myself, and tried to act like I wasn't nervous. Lee was dressed in a maroon V-neck sweater and eyeglasses with thick black frames. He smiled and waved for me and my manager, John, to take a seat while he finished up a phone call.

I was meeting with Lee because Jon Radler, an exec at Imagine Entertainment, which coproduced *Empire*, had heard me on a podcast and thought me and Lee might click. Except for the time I was on *Judge Joe Brown*, I'd never been on the set of a TV show before, and now here I was, meeting with the director of one of the hottest shows on prime-time TV.

Months earlier, not long after all those white boys put me on their podcasts, my manager started getting calls from Hollywood people who wanted to "bring my story to the screen." I had meetings in offices in Burbank and Century City and in fancy restaurants where nobody ate the food except me. I met with producers from companies I'd never heard of and executives who worked on shows I loved, like *The Bernie Mac Show* and *Orange Is the New Black*.

Every meeting would start the same: Somebody would ask me to talk about my life. I'd tell them stories about growing up poor in Atlanta, having two babies by the time I was fifteen, selling drugs and forging checks, then moving to a lily-white suburb of Indianapolis. They'd listen, eyes wide, with their full attention, laughing at all my jokes. One person said, "You're so brave," which was the stupidest shit I ever heard. There's nothing "brave" about being born into poverty. It's not like I had a choice.

At the end of every meeting, there were handshakes and hugs. They'd say, "We can't wait to circle back!" or, "Let's continue the conversation!" or, "So excited to work with you!" But when my manager called to follow up, an assistant to the assistant to the second assistant's assistant would deliver the message that this or that executive had decided to "take a pass." I was confused as hell.

Where I come from, nobody gives you compliments unless they want something. And if they have some shit to say, they'll say it to your face. Hollywood, I discovered, is the exact opposite. Folks will praise you to the heavens for no damn reason. And if they have a negative comment, you won't hear it from them. They'll pay an assistant to say it.

When I sat down with Lee Daniels, I was expecting him to do what everybody in Hollywood did—tell me that my story was "raw" and "gritty" and blah blah blah. Instead, he surprised the hell outta me. This man wanted to tell me about himself.

He didn't get to Hollywood through connections, like a lot of other folks. He started at the bottom and worked his way up.

Lee was raised in West Philadelphia with his five siblings and his mama. His daddy died when he was twelve. He dropped out of college and moved to LA with only seven dollars in his pocket. He stole food when he was hungry. He got into drugs. He was homeless for a while. But like me, he's a hustler. He got a job at a nursing agency. Then he started running his own agency. By the time he was twenty-two, his company was worth millions. He sold it to follow his passion. That's how he started making movies.

I respected Lee's come-up. But I was even more impressed that he seemed to have a golden touch. The first movie he produced was *Monster's Ball.* He cast Halle Berry as the lead. She became the first Black woman to ever win a Best Actress Academy Award. I remember watching that ceremony with Michael, back in Riverdale. When they opened the envelope and called Halle's name, I went crazy, hollering at the TV like our own sister had won.

Lee worked with Halle, Taraji, and Mo'Nique, which told me that Black women trust him. He'd cast Gabourey, who'd never acted before, in the starring role in *Precious*, which meant he was willing to work with beginners. Most of all, I appreciated that when we talked, Lee didn't try to gas me up. He was straightforward as hell. *Finally*, I thought, *a nigga who isn't tryna bullshit me.* Lee felt like somebody I could trust.

"Look," he said, "you're gonna meet a lot of folks in this business who do things a certain way. But I'm from the streets. We have a lot in common." Then he got to the point. He said there were too many similarities between my story and his movie *Precious*. "I feel like I've already done this," he added, looking me dead in the eye. "I'm not sure why I would want to tell this same story again."

This wasn't the first time someone had compared my life to *Precious*. It never made sense to me. That movie is depressing as hell. It's about a teenage girl named Precious living on welfare and Section 8 with her abusive mama. She has two babies by her own daddy, who also gave her HIV. The movie tells the story of Precious learning how to read. Or some shit. I'm not sure. I didn't tell Lee, but I never saw *Precious* myself. Who the hell wants to go to a movie just to feel sad?

In his trailer, I told Lee the same thing I'd said every time somebody brought this up. "*Precious* is *not* my story," I insisted. "If you got two Black women who get punched in the eye, those two punches hit different. We don't get dragged down the street the same; we don't get abused the same. Also," I added, "I been reading since third grade. So, it's not the same story at all."

I reminded Lee that I'm a comic. I wanted to make a sitcom. I'd been dreaming about it ever since I did my first open mic. "I want audiences to know that no matter how bad things are, you can always find a laugh," I said.

I told Lee that even though I grew up poor in Atlanta, got pregnant young, sold drugs, forged checks, and went to jail, I was currently living with my happy family in a middle-class suburb so white it was like somebody threw a family of raisins into a jar of mayonnaise. I also mentioned that I was raising my third set of kids. "They my crack babies," I said. "Because they mama *and* they grandmama is on crack." He listened and nodded and laughed a few times, which I took as a good sign.

I thought the meeting went well. But I knew a "good meeting" doesn't mean shit in Hollywood.

I flew back home to Michael and the kids. A few weeks later, my manager John called to let me know that Lee Daniels wanted to make a sitcom, starring me.

The deal—a partnership between Lee Daniels, Fox TV, and Imagine Entertainment—was to develop a show based on my life and comedy. I was going to get a creator and executive producer credit. As John described the terms of the deal, I held the phone to my ear, trying to take it all in. This was bigger than my wildest dreams: I had an Academy Award–winning director, a giant production company, and a huge TV network behind me. I should have been excited. But deep down, I was terrified.

I knew I had good stories to tell, and I knew I could tell a joke. But when it came to everything else, I was in way over my head. I didn't know the first thing about acting. Or television. Or writing no damn script. I had no experience, no training, no education in the field. I felt like a total fraud.

But then I thought about how I was living at seventeen. Back then, I'd go to the mall with stolen checks and a fake ID, pretending I was rich as hell as I shopped for big-screen TVs and designer clothes. If I could run that game as a teenager, then I could pass myself off as an executive producer and star of my very own TV show.

The way it was explained to me, getting a TV show on the air sounded pretty straightforward. First, you needed to figure out a concept for the show and write a script for the pilot episode. If the script was accepted by the execs at Imagine and Fox, we'd get a green light to shoot the pilot. If the execs liked the pilot, and it tested well with focus groups, then Fox might buy the show and turn it into a series. As far as I could tell, everything depended on that pilot script. If it was good, things would flow like melted butter.

Since I'd never worked in television before, the studio execs arranged for me to work with a professional TV writer. The show was going to be based on my life. I figured all they'd need to do was ask me about my life in Indianapolis with Michael and the kids, add some jokes from my stand-up and some stories from my book, *Rabbit*. Once they mixed it all together, they'd have a perfect script. I'm not a writer, but it sounded like easy work to me.

The first writer the studio paired me up with was cool. But we didn't click at all. Then they put me with someone else. But that didn't work out, either.

The studio had sent me writers with a lot of experience working on successful sitcoms, like that was a good thing. But I was beginning to wonder if maybe their experience *was* the problem. Instead of taking inspiration from my life, they kept writing scripts that sounded like TV shows I've seen before. In one script, the writer had me playing a big-boned Black woman with a sassy attitude and a job as an in-home medical aide. In another, my character was a big-boned Black woman with a sassy attitude, but this time I worked in an office. There were no versions of the show that featured a Black mother and wife living in the suburbs who also happened to be an ex–drug dealer, convicted felon, and touring stand-up comedian. I guess they thought it would be impossible for Middle America to accept that a comedian could also be a good mom.

It would have been easy for me to agree to some whack-ass idea just to get my show on the air. But I wanted something real. Not just for me but also for Black TV history.

I noticed that Black male comics like Redd Foxx, Bill Cosby, Chris Rock, Bernie Mac, Steve Harvey, D. L. Hughley, Martin Lawrence, and Damon Wayans had all starred in sitcoms based on their lives or their comedy. But when it came to Black women stand-ups, we rarely had that chance. Mo'Nique starred in *The Parkers*, Wanda Sykes starred in *Wanda at Large*, and stand-up comic Thea Vidale starred in her own sitcom, *Thea*, on ABC. But all these shows had been off the air for more than twenty years. It felt like the TV industry was telling Black women comedians, *Nobody cares about your stories, and nobody is interested in your life*. I thought if I could get my show on the air, it would break the cycle.

Everybody knows you only get so many chances in Hollywood. After two failed attempts at a script, I was scared that Fox was going to kill my dream before it even had a chance to be born. I lay in bed one night and prayed to God to send me a writer who could help me get my story on TV. *It's not just for me*, I told God. *It's for Black history*. I felt like God was up in heaven rolling his eyes, like *Girl, please. I got wars and famines to deal with. You need to figure this shit out on your own.*

Lee Daniels also wanted to find the perfect writer. He told me that instead of looking for someone in Hollywood, he was going to "take this search to the streets." A few weeks later, he called to tell me there was a young playwright in New York he thought I should meet.

On April 1, 2018, Lee flew me from Iowa, where I was doing a weekend gig at the Funny Bone in West Des Moines, to New York City, to see *Ain't No Mo'* at the Public Theater. The play was about Black folks in America going back to Africa because they were sick and tired of racism. It was hilarious but also full of big ideas.

The next morning, I met Jordan E. Cooper, who wrote and starred in the play, for breakfast. Lee had told me that Jordan was a Hollywood outsider, with no industry experience. What he didn't tell me was that Jordan was twenty-two years old and still in college. He didn't have TV experience because they don't give TV writer jobs to folks fresh out the womb.

We met in a little restaurant on the Lower East Side, which I guess is where students hang out, because I did not see one person close to my age. Jordan was wearing some shiny Nikes that made him look like he had cartoon character feet. I got there early and ordered a coffee. He sat down across from me and gave me a wide smile.

"I like your play," I told him. "It feels like you were here before. You write like in a past life you were a big Black woman."

He threw his head back and laughed. "I don't know what that means," he said. "But thank you."

I asked Jordan how he came up with the idea for his play. He told me about a night two years earlier when he was in a 7-Eleven buying a Slurpee. A police officer walked into the store, took one look at Jordan, and put his hand on his gun. "This happened not long after Philando Castile and Alton Sterling," Jordan said. "And it got me thinking about how much a Black life is worth." That hit me hard. I remember when those two unarmed Black men were shot dead by police in a single week. It made me afraid for my two sons.

I liked that Jordan was a deep thinker. I liked him even more when he told me why he was convinced that "it was fate" that we would meet.

The year before, he'd seen me on Harry Connick Jr.'s talk show, talking about my book *Rabbit*. Jordan was a broke college student. He couldn't afford thirty-five dollars for a hardcover book. He saved a screenshot of the book jacket in his phone as a reminder to buy it when he had the funds. He pulled out his phone to show me.

Flash forward a year, when Lee Daniels came out to watch a workshop of Jordan's play. "He told me he was working with a comedian to develop a TV show," said Jordan. "He said I should 'read her memoir' to see if I had any ideas." Jordan said when he found out that the book Lee wanted him to read was *Rabbit*, it felt like destiny.

Before we met, Jordan read *Rabbit* cover to cover. He listened to me on podcasts and watched clips of my stand-up online. He knew my whole life story. His idea for my TV show was to make the main character a stand-up comic. "We've never seen a Black woman comedian and her family portrayed on TV before," he said. "Plus, it gives us an opportunity to show a Black man holding it down at home while his working wife is on the road. We haven't seen that on TV, either." Jordan said he wanted to use the stories in *Rabbit* as a "road map" to help create the main character. He even had a working title in mind. "It should be called *The Ms. Pat Show*," he said.

When the studio put me with writers, they'd always send me CVs and résumés listing their qualifications. But I'm not a résumé person. I go by feelings; I trust my gut. It didn't matter to me if Jordan was a twenty-two-year-old still-in-college student with zero TV experience. My spirit said, *He's the one*.

CHAPTER 19

SHOWTIME

I told Lee that I loved Jordan and wanted to hire him as the writer. When Lee brought the idea to the studio folks, they said abso-fucking-lutely not. It was bad enough that *I* didn't know what I was doing. They sure as hell didn't want a tag team of two people who'd never worked in the industry before—especially when one of them dropped out in eighth grade and the other was still in college.

In Hollywood, studio execs will *say* they want fresh talent and new ideas. But it's damn near impossible to actually get them to give fresh talent and new ideas a chance. They don't get excited about people they don't know. They get worried.

Lee said the studio was going to find me another "qualified" writer, which is exactly what I didn't want.

"Don't even worry about them muthafuckas," I told Jordan when I called to give him the bad news. The studio had said no to hiring Jordan as a writer. But I decided to ignore them. My plan was for the two of us to write an excellent script and have Lee submit it to the execs for approval. If they liked it, I figured they'd have to hire Jordan for the job. "But we want them to read it with an open mind," I said. "So you gotta take your name off the script when we hand it in."

There was a pause on the other end of the line.

I knew that asking a writer not to claim their work was a crazy request. But we needed to be strategic: when you're trying to break into a members-only club, you can't expect folks to fling the gates wide open. Sometimes you gotta sneak around and pick the backdoor lock.

Jordan's not stupid. He knew what we were up against. "I'm not going to steal your script," I promised. "If it gets accepted, we'll put your name right back on."

We didn't have a lot of time. That same night, we got right to work. Or I should say, Jordan got to work, writing around the clock. My job was to answer his questions whenever he called and to do my best to hype him up.

Jordan would ask things like, "What would you do if your child was in a fight at school?" or, "How do you talk to your adult son who still lives at home?" Then he'd take whatever I told him and mix it in with everything he'd read in my book *Rabbit* and heard in my comedy. To keep him motivated, I'd call him bright and early at 6 a.m. "We're running out of time," I'd yell into the phone. "Write, nigga, write!" I thought I was being helpful. Then Jordan put his phone on Do Not Disturb.

The two of us was like puppies chasing a ball: all excitement and no training. Jordan didn't even have Final Draft, the software TV people use to write scripts. He used Microsoft Word, like he was writing an essay for school. I ordered Jordan Final Draft on my credit card and Cash Apped him some money to buy groceries so he wouldn't starve.

Two weeks after our first meeting, Jordan sent me a finished script. My character, Patricia Carson, a stand-up comedian, comes home after a weekend gig to find out that her daughter, Janelle, got into a physical altercation at her mostly white high school. The fight started as an argument about school shootings and race. Meanwhile, my character's younger son Junebug is busy posting all kinds of crazy shit on social media. Including his sister's WorldStar fight. Her oldest son is a knucklehead who lives in the basement and plays video games all day.

That shit was so good, it was like I was reading about my real life. Every sentence my character said felt like it came straight out of my own head. If anything, it was almost *too* real. "Why is there so much damn cussing?" I asked Jordan. "Nigga, I don't even muthafuckin' talk like that."

Jordan said he wanted my show to be authentic. That meant my character needed to speak like me. "Maybe you can't hear it," he added. "But you cuss *a lot*. You're the queen of cussing."

I was in my kitchen, talking to Jordan on speakerphone. Michaela was sitting at the table, listening in. When Jordan explained how important it was to capture the realness of my family life, Michaela said, "What Jordan is trying to do is revolutionary. You need to listen to him." Michaela was still in high school, but she's the smartest of all my kids. If she thought Jordan was on to something, then I figured I should go along. That's how "nigga this" and "nigga that" and every cussword combination you can think of ended up sprinkled on every single muthafuckin' page.

I showed Jordan's script to Lee. He said it was great. "But who wrote this?" he asked. "I know it wasn't you because everything is spelled correctly."

Lee passed the script on to the executives. They loved it, just like I knew they would. The only problem was the nonstop cussing. They said the language was too spicy for network TV. So Fox sold the show to Hulu. The streamer had never done a multi-cam sitcom before. *The Ms. Pat Show* was going to be its first.

In the summer of 2019, we went into production. Lee showed the script to Debbie Allen—*the* Debbie Allen, who's directed everything from *A Different World* to *Grey's Anatomy*. I almost passed out from excitement when Lee said that Debbie had agreed to direct the pilot. She'd directed Will Smith in his first-ever acting gig, the pilot of *The Fresh Prince of Bel-Air*, which meant she knew how to support first-time actors. I knew I'd be safe with her.

Debbie Allen has been acting, producing, and directing for more than four decades. She's one of the most accomplished women in television. But when we met with execs from Hulu to discuss directors, Jordan mentioned Debbie's name and someone from the Hulu team asked, "Who is she?" That was the first sign of trouble.

In television, things move as slow as molasses and then suddenly speed up. It had taken more than a year to get the pilot green-lit. But once that happened, everything started moving way too fast.

We got our green light at the end of July; we were scheduled to shoot the pilot six weeks later. But before that happened, Jordan told me we had one more hurdle to cross. He said I had to kill at the table read. I didn't even know what the hell a table read was.

A table read, or "read-through," is when the whole cast sits at a big table like the Last Supper and reads through their lines in front of a roomful of studio execs. A show can live or die depending on how the table read goes.

A pilot for a multi-cam sitcom can cost between one and a half million and three million dollars to make. The studio pays for everything: casting all the characters, building the sets, hiring the director and all the crew. Before they lay out all that money, they need to know that the show has the potential to be a hit. The table read is their chance to check the progress and see if there is anything they want to change. It's TV judgment day. As in, the executives get *real* judgy.

They watch, take notes, then talk among themselves: Is the show funny? Did the script have enough laughs? Are the characters likable?

Do the actors have charisma? If they don't like what they see, the execs might send the script back for a rewrite, or hire a different writer, or fire all the actors and recast all their roles. In a worst-case scenario, they'll cancel the whole show.

For a sitcom in development, the table read is a do-or-die situation. With so much at stake, I had to get it right, which meant I needed to practice. So Jordan and I organized a fake table read behind the studio's back. We flew out to Los Angeles. Jordan invited a bunch of his actor friends, and I invited a couple of comics, and we all met up in a conference room at my manager's office on Sunset Boulevard.

The thing about a table read is that it isn't just reading; you have to say the lines *in character*. If my character is mad on the page, I needed to be mad at the table read. There's acting involved. I'd spent fifteen years developing my skills as a comedian. I didn't know a damn thing about acting.

At the fake table read, I didn't read my lines in character. There was no emotion in my voice. I didn't know that when there was a question mark at the end of a sentence, it meant my voice should go up. I didn't realize that when I saw three dots in the middle of my lines, it was an "ellipsis," and that meant I should pause for dramatic effect. I was focusing hard, running my finger under the words like I did in elementary school. When I glanced up and locked eyes with my friend Vince Bryant, a comic from Atlanta, he looked like he was trying hard not to laugh.

After the table read, I asked Vince how I did. I wanted an honest answer, and comics tell it like it is.

"Well, you definitely weren't good," he said, "at all."

"It was really that bad?"

"Put it this way," he added. "They're probably gonna make this show . . . I just don't know if they're going to put you in it."

The next day, I signed up for acting classes.

My acting coach, Kevin Benton, was a no-nonsense instructor from the Tasha Smith Actors Workshop. Kevin explained that acting is more than reciting words on a page. He said I had to listen and then *react* to whatever the other character said. I practiced and practiced and practiced some more. I slept with that damn script under my pillow. I tried to *feel* the dialogue and act with genuine emotion. But mostly, what I did was count.

They don't teach this method in acting class. I came up with it on my own. I'd say my line and then count in my head the twenty-seven words that J. Bernard Calloway, the actor who was playing my husband, was supposed to say before Tami Roman, the actor who was playing my sister, Denise, came in with her nineteen. I wasn't acting. It was more like waiting for my turn to talk. I learned a long time ago that when I learn a new life skill, sometimes I have to fake it until the real skill catches up.

A month and a half later, in August, me, Jordan, Debbie Allen, Lee Daniels, the main cast and supporting actors, and fifty-eight Hulu, Fox, and Imagine executives dressed in button-down shirts and expensive shoes met in a large room on the Fox Studio Lot. Debbie Allen and the cast sat at the long conference table at the front of the room. The execs sat in chairs right up under our noses. Seated behind them was Vince. He was there to give me moral support. I'm used to performing onstage. But this was different. I felt like an animal in the zoo.

I scanned my memory, trying to recall everything my acting coach had told me: *listen, respond, feel the emotion*. But it was only after the execs laughed at one of my jokes that I finally felt myself relax.

"You really did your thing," Vince said when we were done. "Because that was some kind of miracle."

And then, a month later, there I was, standing onstage in front of a live studio audience, getting ready to shoot my pilot with a spotlight shining bright in my face.

The pilot of *The Ms. Pat Show* was shot on Stage 20 at the Fox Studio Lot in Century City, Los Angeles. Jordan, who's like a walking encyclopedia of TV knowledge, told me that us being in this space was symbolic. In 1968, Diahann Carroll shot *Julia* on this very same soundstage. She became the first Black woman to star in a network series where the Black woman wasn't playing a maid. *Julia* featured Diahann as a beautiful nurse with a bad-ass wardrobe. The show became a huge hit. But for some Black folks it also felt like a slap in the face. The show aired the same year Dr. Martin Luther King Jr. was assassinated, but Julia seemed to live in a world where racism didn't exist. This wasn't *our* reality. It was a whitewashed version of Blackness. As Diahann put it, the show was "presenting the white Negro." When Diahann wanted her character to rock an Afro, the show's white producers told her no.

Now, here I was fifty-one years later, making a show about a Black woman and her family that was authentic, uncompromising, and there wasn't nothing white about it.

Jordan wanted every episode of *The Ms. Pat Show* to open with a few minutes of me, alone onstage, holding a mic, doing stand-up. The night we shot our pilot, I could feel the audience buzzing with energy as I delivered my very first line. "Any of you muthafuckas ever been shot before?" I asked, staring out into the crowd. "I have. Twice!"

In the first three minutes of our first-ever show, we talked about gun violence, school shootings, racism, and police brutality. Just like my caseworker Ms. Campbell had said years before, we took all that pain and made it funny.

That night was perfect. The cast and crew were on point. The audience laughed so loud they almost drowned out my lines. At the end of the shoot, I gave a little speech. "I want to thank my husband, Michael, for holding me down all these years," I said. "I love you." Michael, who was sitting in the stands with all our kids, put his head in his hands so none of them would see his eyes fill with tears.

The pilot was everything I'd dreamed it would be, true to my life and my comedy, and unlike anything else on TV. That night should have been one of the happiest times of my life. But my spirit told me something wasn't right.

Earlier that day, before we started taping, I'd asked Vince, who was on set helping out, to sneak into the room where all the Hulu execs were watching us on a giant TV monitor. "Don't say nothing," I'd told him. "Just hang back and listen to what they say."

After we wrapped for the night, the cast and crew were hanging out on set, eating pizza and taking photos. Vince found me and gave me his report. "It's not good," he said, shaking his head. According to Vince, the big boss man from Hulu—the shot caller in charge of programming—hadn't laughed at one single joke. "Not even the one about the thumb in the ass?" I asked.

"Nah."

"What about 'It's bedtime in Africa'?"

"Nope."

"Not even 'boo nigga boo'?"

"Nothing," he said.

The Hulu execs didn't get my comedy or understand why the show was important. They didn't know that there were people who'd want to see a show like mine because it feels like home. It was frustrating as hell. But not a total surprise. For weeks, the folks at Hulu had been giving whack-ass notes to Jordan, like "Why is the mother always yelling?" and "How come her twenty-eight-year-old son still lives at home?" It was like they wanted a show about a Black family, but not if that Black family was like mine.

Hulu wasn't interested in moving the pilot to series. But for six months, they also didn't officially cancel our deal. It was like being in a bad marriage with someone who won't sign the divorce papers.

Then, on Valentine's Day 2020, I was at the Improv in Raleigh, North Carolina, about to step onstage to do my set when Lee Daniels's number came up on my phone. He was calling to let me know that Hulu had finally terminated the deal. "I'm so sorry," he said.

"It's okay," I told him. And I really meant it. I've been getting rejections my whole life. To me, a no doesn't mean it's over. "No" just means "find another way."

After Hulu canceled our deal, Lee sent *The Ms. Pat Show* pilot all over the damn place—to Netflix, Amazon Prime, FX—looking for another streamer to buy the show. One studio said they "already had a Black show." Another told us they "didn't get it." The third place wanted to know if we'd be open to changing the names of my TV children because they thought "Janelle" sounded "too ethnic." The only streamer to offer us a deal was BET+. I didn't even know BET had a plus.

Jordan was crushed. He thought we should be someplace with a higher profile so we'd get more eyeballs on the show. But I told him not to worry. As a drug dealer, I learned that location is not as important as having a quality product. "There's two things you'll never see a commercial for," I told him. "Waffle House and crack. That's because the product sells itself. If the show is good, the audience will come." I told Jordan to forget about Hulu and Netflix and all the places that rejected us. "In this life," I said, "you gotta fuck with the people who fuck with you and stop running after the ones who don't."

Not long after we signed our deal with BET+, I was home with Michael, drinking my morning coffee. He was going through the mail. He opened a letter and frowned. I glanced over his shoulder to see what he was reading. At the top of the page, in bold print, it said "Notice of Loan Maturity and Balloon Payment Due."

For fifteen years, Michael had been paying $226 a month on that janky-ass home-equity interest-only loan we got back in Riverdale. But that month, when Michael sent in his check, the bank returned it with a notice explaining that the fifteen-year term of the loan was up.

We'd borrowed $27,800 in 2005. Since then, Michael had paid the bank a total of $40,680, in $226 monthly installments. But that only covered the *interest* on the loan. We still owed the full amount we'd borrowed: $27,800.

"'If the default is not cured on or before thirty days from the date of this notice,'" Michael read aloud from the page, "'the lender will accelerate the entire indebtedness and may proceed with foreclosure of the property in accordance with applicable law.'"

"What's that mean?" I asked.

"I think it's saying if we don't pay that money in full, the bank is going to foreclose on the house." Michael was beside himself. "Pat, we don't have that type of money," he said.

For all the years we'd been together, Michael had always been the one to hold us down. He'd paid all the bills; he helped me raise all those kids; he bailed me out of jail, more than once. He stood by me when I buried us under a mountain of debt and loved me through every bad decision. Every time I charged ahead without thinking, he'd been there to clean up the mess. Thanks to my TV deal, for the first time ever, *I* could be the one to bail us out.

"Don't worry about any of that," I told him. "Fuck the bank. I can pay them off right now. We good." Seeing the relief on Michael's face was one of the sweetest sights I've ever known.

CHAPTER 20

WORDS MATTER

After a sitcom gets picked up, a team of writers gets together in a "writers' room" to hash out ideas for plots and storylines for the entire season. The showrunner assigns each episode to a writer. That writer will bang out a first draft. Then everybody comes back together to add jokes or tweak a storyline or make other suggestions to help improve the script. Usually, writers' rooms meet in person. But *The Ms. Pat Show* got picked up in October 2020, and everybody was still scared of COVID-19, so our room met over Zoom.

Some of the writers were folks me and Jordan hired because we knew them and trusted their comedy instincts, including my daughter Michaela and my friend Vince. But none of us, including me and Jordan, had ever worked on a TV show before. So the studio made us hire a professional showrunner and a couple of writers with years of TV experience.

One of these writers—I'll call her Gretchen—had worked on all kinds of sitcoms, including a very successful kids' show. She had a great reputation. But when I read the script she'd written, I damn near lost my mind.

The dialogue was supposed to sound like me, but the words were nothing I would ever say. In one scene, Gretchen had my character saying, "Carpe diem!"

"What the fuck is a 'carpe diem'?" I asked.

"It's Latin," Michaela explained. "It means 'seize the day.'"

"Sneeze the day? What's that mean?"

"*Seize*," said Michaela. "Like, go for it. Grab the day by the balls."

"Take that out," I said. "Why the fuck would a character based on my life know Latin? That's the stupidest shit I ever heard."

The next day in the writers' room, I continued giving Gretchen my opinion. "This script isn't funny," I said. "It's the most unfunny shit I ever read. And it don't fit the show."

That was my main feedback. But I was so stressed-out, I might have also called her a no-talent heifer. I can't remember the specifics. Whatever I said, Gretchen didn't like it. Jordan and I rewrote her script. She didn't like that, either.

A few days later, we were talking through an episode about my TV daughter coming out as gay. Someone in the room said we should make the character bisexual. I said, hell no. I wanted my TV daughter to be a regular lesbian, like my real daughter, Ashley. "I don't want no bisexual or try sexual or any other combination," I said. I thought the writers might be inspired if I told a story about my own daughter coming out.

"We didn't talk for a long time because Ashley was scared that I wouldn't accept her," I told them. "But I said to her, 'I don't care who you be fucking and sucking. You family and we'll always love you.' Then I said, 'But if you come over here to eat, you better bring your own knife and fork. I don't want no pussy juice on my silverware.'" That story was so funny to me. In the writers' room, I laughed my ass off. I figured since they were working on an episode about coming out, they might want to include it in the script.

Apparently, Gretchen did *not* find my story amusing. She went straight to HR and filed a complaint. She called me "homophobic" and accused me of creating a "hostile work environment." I was so mad, I wanted to stomp that chick to the ground.

How the hell was she calling the environment "hostile" when we're meeting over Zoom? *You're sitting in your own apartment*, I wanted to tell her. *Maybe* you're *the hostile environment*? And I damn sure wasn't homophobic, either. I *used* to be homophobic. But I'm not anymore. Of all Gretchen's complaints, that one hurt the most.

When I was younger, I really and truly thought there was something wrong with you if you were gay, because that's what I'd been taught. I heard it in all the different churches Mama dragged me to on Sundays after she found out she could get free food from the church pantry if we sat through the sermon. I heard it from my granddaddy, who'd call certain men "sissies," or worse. I heard it from my daddy, who said being gay is "an unholy sin." I even heard it from Ms. Campbell, my caseworker at the Clayton County Welfare-to-Work program who became my good friend. When I told her my daughter was gay, Ms. Campbell closed her eyes, held my hands in hers, and told me we should pray the gay away.

Ashley knew she was gay in high school. But I refused to believe it. I was in so much denial that even when I caught her reading E. Lynn Harris, studying those pages like it was her bible, I still didn't catch on. But Michael's mama did.

"I was at your mama's today," I told Michael one night when the two of us was in bed. "She said Ashley has a gay spirit. So I told her that her wig had a gay spirit 'cause it ain't straight, either." I was so mad. It felt like his mama was insulting me. "Ashley is *not* gay," I insisted.

"Pat, it's not your choice," Michael said. "You need to let her be."

It must have been so hard for my daughter back then, trying to figure out who she was while listening to her own mama talking all kinds of ugly gay-hating shit around the house. When Ashley finished high school, she went off to college. I thought she was studying business, but now I think maybe she just wanted to get away from me and start living her best gay life out loud. When she dropped out of college a year later, instead of coming home, Ashley moved to Virginia to live with some friends. For almost three years, we barely talked. It hurt my heart to know that my own child didn't feel welcome in the family home all because of me.

I knew that if I wanted Ashley back in our lives, I needed to get over my bullshit and let my daughter know that she was loved.

I reached out to her on Facebook and told her we needed to talk.

"You gay?" I asked when she finally called. "You can tell me. Because I already know, and I don't care. I support you. In fact, I think you should be the biggest baddest lesbian there is. Please, Ashley, you need to come on home."

I feel bad that it took me having a gay daughter before I realized that being anti-gay was hateful and ignorant as hell. But we all have our own journeys out of the darkness and into the light. Realizing I might lose my firstborn child is how I came to my senses.

Now, I'm proud to say my daughter is a lesbian. And she ain't no run-of-the-mill lesbian, either. She's a top-shelf gold-star gay. She's the Michael Jordan of pussy eating. Just like any parent, I'm happy my child is good at what she does.

When Gretchen called me homophobic, it felt like she was accusing me of an anti-gay crime when I already did my time in homophobia rehabilitation.

The more I thought about what Gretchen said, the angrier I became. Because how the hell are you reporting me to HR for being myself on my own damn TV show? This type of nonsense doesn't happen in comedy clubs. With comics, nobody's worried about anybody's feelings. It's free and easy and everybody just says whatever the fuck they want. As long as it's funny, it don't matter if it hurts. So it surprised the hell outta me when I learned that in TV writers' rooms, you need to watch what you say. If someone gets upset, then all hell breaks loose, and everybody has to run around trying to pacify some grown-ass adult.

The whole situation was so stupid, I thought for sure it would just blow over. I mean, even the HR people had to agree that I hadn't done anything wrong. All I'd done was yell at the bitch and tell her she wasn't any good at her job. My dumbass boss at McDonald's did the same damn thing.

Gretchen had reported me to HR at ten o'clock that morning. By ten o'clock that night, I was exhausted and getting ready to take my ass to bed. I was in my bathroom, buck naked, about to step into the shower, when I got a call from Lee Daniels.

"Hello?"

"I don't know what the fuck you did, Pat," he said. He sounded angry. "The studio is about to cancel your show."

Now I was mad all over again.

"I don't care," I told him. "I didn't do shit to her. I'm a comedian. You can't be no TV writer if you scared of a fucking joke."

"I'm trying to help you," Lee said. "I've been telling these white folks that you been through some shit. I told them that you need counseling."

"But I didn't do nothing," I repeated.

"Pat, you're not hearing me. I'm trying to save your show."

A few days later, Lee called me again. "I've got some good news," he said. The BET execs decided that they'd already sunk too much money into my show to cancel it. We could move forward, he said. But I needed to learn how to calm the hell down. To help me out, the studio had hired me a life coach to teach me anger management and some new communication skills.

Treiva Williams was a young-looking middle-aged Black woman who rocked ginger-colored micro braids, platinum hoop earrings, long flowy skirts, and Jordans. She smiled a lot and told me her job was to help me "navigate challenging situations." I liked her right away. She felt like a sister. Not like my *real* sister. This woman felt like someone I could actually trust.

For our first meeting, we sat in my trailer, just the two of us. "You have a lot riding on the success of your show," Treiva said. "That must feel like a lot of pressure, all the time."

"Yes, it sure do."

Treiva said I needed to create a peaceful environment where I could decompress. "Somewhere you can go for five minutes of quiet in the middle of a hectic day," she explained. She put candles in my trailer and set up a little table in the corner with a miniature rock fountain that made the sound of running water. She asked one of the set electricians to put dimmers on the light switch so I could turn the lights low and create a peaceful vibe. "When you're feeling agitated," she said, "try stepping away from the situation, take ten deep breaths, and see if that helps you calm down."

Then she started on the real work, which was teaching me a new communication style. Before Treiva, I thought I *was* a great communicator. I stood onstage and talked to folks for a living. I knew how to get my point across. But Treiva opened my eyes to what she called "unnecessarily combative interactions." She said, when I get heated, my first instinct is to fight.

"This is a learned pattern that may have been beneficial when you were in the streets," she explained. "But you're working for a corporation now. You have a staff of people who come from different backgrounds. So you may need to adjust your approach."

According to Treiva, I couldn't go around telling people I was finna knock their fucking teeth out just because I was frustrated or didn't think their joke was funny. I also couldn't say, "I hate this. It's stupid. Take it out. The fuck is wrong with you?" Which I thought was just being direct and to the point. But I learned you can't talk like that to folks who have a union.

To help me get the hang of it, Treiva proposed a plan: every time I wanted to cuss someone out, she told me to call her instead. I was dialing her number morning, noon, and night. She'd listen patiently and tell me to take a beat. Then she'd translate what I was saying into different phrases I could use. For instance, instead of saying, "This script ain't funny for shit," I was supposed to say, "Is there another way we can do this?" or, "How about you take another pass?"

At first, it felt like Treiva was teaching me to be fake and phony like so many people I'd met in Hollywood, instead of my authentic self. But I've come to realize that cussing folks out with the full force of my frustration isn't very productive in the workplace. It doesn't make the person any funnier. It just gets me reported to HR.

With the life I've lived, I didn't think anyone could teach me shit about thriving and surviving. I thought the skills I used to get me this far would serve me well forever. But I've learned that the strategies that help you on a journey might be different from the skills you need when you arrive. That's the beauty of moving forward in life. You learn and grow along the way.

In the first season of *The Ms. Pat Show*, we tackled race, class, generational trauma, addiction, and abuse. We didn't turn away from difficult topics, and we didn't clean up the language. Some folks said the way I cussed out my TV family felt "liberating." Other people thought the show was too spicy, too vulgar, and that I was too damn rude. On Twitter, somebody asked what kind of people would call their own children the N-word? First of all, it's not the N-word. When Black folks say it, we put an "a" at the end. It's a whole different word with a different meaning. Our word is not filled with hate. It's an insider thing. Only we get to say it. After all the shit we been through in this country, we get to have whatever the hell word we want. I guess some folks in America need to be better educated about language, history, and culture. Because getting mad about what I call my kids with love and affection was the dumbest shit I ever heard.

In one of my favorite episodes of the first season, my TV daughter Janelle brings home her nonbinary friend Jesse. At first, my character, like a lot of folks of my generation, struggles to get the pronouns right. I'm so confused, I refer to the child as "him," then "her," then I give up and call them "that nigga." But by the end of the show, my character has totally come around, standing up for Jesse and cursing out their closed-minded mama.

"Your mama's a bitch," my character tells Jesse when their mother shows up at my front door. "You can come over anytime, just don't bring her ass!" I got a lot of love from my LGBTQIA+ fans for that. A few kids put the scene on TikTok. The comments lit up with appreciation for the way my character started off ignorant, then came around to the truth. Every child deserves love and respect from their parents, no matter if they're straight, gay, trans, or wear their Crocs in sports mode.

BET took a chance on us when other networks turned us away. In the end, BET+ came out on top. *The Ms. Pat Show* premiered August 12,

2021, and quickly became the highest-rated show on the streamer. So many people logged on to watch the first episode, it almost crashed the app.

The first season of *The Ms. Pat Show* made history as the first BET scripted series to ever get nominated for a Primetime Emmy Award. BET has been around for four decades; it took my show to finally break through. That year, I went to the Emmys dressed in a royal-blue silk floor-length gown covered in brocade. That dress was so poufy, I looked like I worked in the kitchen on *Game of Thrones*.

Our show was nominated for Outstanding Directing for a Comedy Series for the episode "Baby Daddy Groundhog Day," directed by Mary Lou Belli. We were up against some of the most popular comedies on TV, including *Atlanta*, *Only Murders in the Building*, and *Ted Lasso*. I didn't feel like I belonged in the same category as Steve Martin and Donald Glover. But I guess God and the Television Academy wanted me to stop doubting myself, because *The Ms. Pat Show* received a second Emmy Award nomination the following year and a third one the year after that.

The Ms. Pat Show has given a lot of new talent a chance to shine. Jordan made a name for himself as the youngest showrunner in TV history. In 2022, his play *Ain't No Mo'* went up on Broadway and was nominated for six Tony Awards. That same year, BET gave me a production deal to star in and produce my own shows. My first project was *Ms. Pat Settles It*, where I listen to people argue about money, bad wigs, and missed car payments, and decide which one of them is right. Only in America can an ex-convict grow up to become a judge on TV.

It's not easy to climb the ladder of success. Especially when you start your journey in the basement. It's even harder when no one believes in your dream except you. When I first started doing comedy, I thought I had a God-given talent because that's what my caseworker, Ms. Campbell, told me. But not everybody agreed.

Back when we was living in Riverdale, I took Ashley with me to some of those early shows. "You were horrible," she said. My own child thought my comedy was trash. My husband didn't think it was worth his time to come out and see me perform. A total stranger was so sure I wasn't going to be funny he threw a Nerf ball in my face before I even told my first joke. In the beginning, it wasn't easy. All I had was a dream that one day I'd make it big. For a lot of years, I carried that dream alone.

In this country, they like to say that anyone can make it. But really, success is like a private club. They don't fling the gates open for everybody. You might need to fight your way in. I hustled and schemed and did all kinds of things folks told me weren't allowed. I made mistakes. I lost my temper. I got impatient. I said things that got me in a whole lot of trouble. Other things I said won me a whole lot of fans.

I'm not one to hold grudges. But there are some things that happened in those early days that I'll never forget. When I was just starting out, a comic I really respected promised me a chance to do a guest spot on a Valentine's Day show he was doing at the Pageant, a big theater in St. Louis.

I was so excited; I'd never played a theater before. The comic said he couldn't pay for my travel, but he knew I was hungry for stage time and I'd get myself wherever I needed to be. I booked a flight on Southwest and put a hotel room on Michael's credit card. It was the dead of winter. The city was covered in snow. At the theater, I found the promoter and introduced myself. "Hi, I'm Ms. Pat," I said, putting my hand out for a shake. I was expecting him to give me a warm welcome and point me to the greenroom. Instead, he just looked me up and down and said, "Who the fuck are you?" I realized then that the comic who'd invited me to perform hadn't told the show's promoter anything about me, which meant there was no chance I was getting on that stage. I left the theater and walked my sorry ass back to my hotel in the Missouri snow, tears rolling down my face.

That shit humbled the hell outta me. But it made me even more determined. Humiliation only breaks you if you let it.

My journey has been full of amazing blessings. I'm able to take my family on wonderful vacations. I was able to retire Michael early. He'll never have to work on an assembly line again. But some of that success came at a cost. For years, I was in the club every night and out on the road all weekend. I missed out on a lot of life back home.

Junebug played football all through high school. I love football. But I hardly made any of his games. In middle school, Michaela competed in the Academic Super Bowl. I don't have no clue what that is. But her team went all the way to the state championship, and I wasn't there to cheer her on. I missed school dances, track meets, parent-teacher conferences, and birthdays.

Even when I was at home, I didn't always do things right.

In Plainfield, we lived in a great school district and a safe neighborhood. I thought my children had everything they needed for a happy life. But white middle-class suburbs have their own set of challenges. Michaela was one of only a few Black girls in her school. And she was a big girl with a lot of opinions, at that. I never talked to her about what that felt like, but one morning I caught her crying. "What's wrong?" I asked. "Are you depressed?"

She nodded yes.

I wanted to protect her. But I'm from the streets, where boo-hooing only makes you a target. In my mind, she needed to toughen up. I told her to pull herself together. "Get over it," I said. I thought I was helping. But now I think maybe I was wrong. Maybe my thirteen-year-old daughter needed a hug and soft words. I don't really know. At that age, I was pregnant and just found out my baby's daddy was married to somebody else. It's hard to parent a child when you never had a childhood yourself.

After that conversation with Michaela, I noticed she kind of clammed up and would only talk to her daddy when she had a problem or needed some advice. I think with Michael she can be open and vulnerable. Those types of conversations are hard for me.

I didn't come from a world where people talked about their feelings. I didn't learn the vocabulary. I knew that a person might feel "damn good" or "mad as hell." But I didn't know shit about those middle-class emotions like feeling "anxious" or "awkward" or "overwhelmed." For me, a "trigger" was something you pulled when you was about to pop a nigga. I thought a "microaggression" was when a little person wanted to fight you. I love Michaela, but sometimes it's like she's talking a different language. I told her, "I know you might not think I'm the best mama. But you should thank me because I gave you the best dad in the world."

It hurts my heart to think that maybe I let my children down. But if I had a chance to do it again, I don't know that I'd do anything different. Because those kids can complain all they want. Meanwhile, they living in my damn house eating up all my food. I worked hard to give them the life I never had.

From the day we first moved to Indiana, I promised myself I'd find a way to get us back to Atlanta. In 2021, I used the money I made on the first season of *The Ms. Pat Show* to buy a house on a seven-acre plot of land in a quiet suburb in Georgia, about a half-hour drive from where I grew up. I tore down the house and built a new twelve-thousand-square-foot, eleven-bedroom, thirteen-bathroom family home from the ground up. I hired a Black woman architect and told her everything I wanted—an open kitchen, twenty-foot ceilings in the living room, an elevator because I don't like taking the stairs. I got my decorating ideas for wallpaper, lighting fixtures, and kitchen faucets from TikTok. Junebug has his own space in the basement. My three nieces have bedrooms on the second floor. I built Michaela her own little house on the property, right next door to ours.

After Michael retired, he got himself three big-ass dogs. His pets live in an eight-hundred-square-foot doghouse out back. It has a wide-screen TV, a built-in washer and dryer, and central air. If ten-year-old me went to sleep and woke up in that doghouse, I would have thought that I'd died and gone to heaven.

Years ago, when owning a home was my biggest goal in life, a trucker with a spider bite told me the American dream was nothing but a lie. I wish I knew where that trucker was now. I want to tell him he was wrong.

When I was little, all I wanted was a safe place to lay my head at night and enough food that I'd never go hungry. When I became a mama, my dream was to give my children the safety and stability that I never had when I was young. As I became successful, I started thinking about the future I wanted for my children, just like the Trucker had talked about all those years before.

Only I'm not buying McDonald's franchises to pass on. The legacy I want to leave for my children and their children and their children's children is that not one of those kids will ever go to school with an empty belly or without knowing where they'll sleep at night. They won't spend their days struggling to survive.

I was born into a family that for generations only knew welfare, food stamps, Section 8, Goodwill clothes, dirty socks, cockroaches crawling on toothbrushes, shoes that didn't fit, caseworkers, cops, underfunded schools, overcrowded ERs, and eviction notices nailed to the door. Success and stability wasn't supposed to find my family. But that all ended with me.

The next generation of my family will have a chance at a bright future. I've set up savings accounts and college funds. I have property to pass on to my kids when I'm gone.

A few months ago, I added Jamal, Tay-Tay, and D'Sani as authorized users on my American Express so they could start building their credit. Before I gave any of those kids they own cards, Michael sat them down at the kitchen table, took out a bill, and showed them how that shit works. I don't want none of them making the same mistakes that I did when I was young.

It feels like I finally broke the cycle of poverty that had cursed my entire family. I got my American dream, and now my kids will have a chance to chase any dream they want. That's all I ever wanted.

Well, that plus a really nice house.

EPILOGUE

I've learned a lot on my journey to a better life. But nothing has opened my eyes more than being a mama. With every new set of kids I've raised, I've had to grow and change.

The first time I held my daughter Ashley, when I was still a child myself, I thought she looked like a little baby doll. I stared into her eyes and made a promise that I'd treat her good. In my mind, that meant three things: I wouldn't let her go hungry, I'd always dress her nice so she wouldn't get bullied at school, and I'd protect her from getting molested. That was my Good Mama criteria. At fourteen, I didn't know that children need more than that.

Then I met Michael. He taught me how to love.

My son Nikia was five years old and Ashley was almost seven when Michael moved in with us. Like any mama, I wanted to make sure that my kids were well-mannered and well-behaved, so I yelled and cussed when I got angry, and I beat they little asses when they was bad. Michael had a whole different way about him. He let Ashley sit in his lap and play with his beard. He taught Nikia how to read.

Michael was so loving, patient, and kind, I worried that he was a bad influence. "You making those kids soft," I complained.

"They *supposed* to be soft," he said. "They only in first and second grade." Michael showed them tenderness and gave them encouragement. He asked them about their day. He was all about that soft love. The only love I knew was hard. I hollered at my kids and told them they better not cry. I was raising them up to be street soldiers, preparing them for a life of war. Michael made me wonder if maybe that was wrong.

He'd ask me questions that got me thinking, like how come I was always whooping my kids whenever I got frustrated. Or why I called them all kinds of "bitches" and "hos" when I was mad. "You're their mama," he said. "Aren't you supposed to be lifting them up with your words?"

"That's what I'm doing," I insisted.

"So why does it sound like you're tearing them down?"

Michael was such a good daddy. I think that's why God kept bringing more kids into our lives.

Me and Michael got custody of Diamond's four children just as my career was taking off and I was beginning to make some money. Those kids got to enjoy all kinds of comfort and privileges growing up. They've never been hungry. They've always lived in excellent school districts. They've flown first class to Hawaii and Belize. Sometimes, I look at them and think, *These kids are so damn lucky to be growing up without a care in the world.* I was sure that kids with money didn't have no problems. But that's what everybody who grows up poor thinks. I've learned that rich kids have problems, too. Just not ones I understand.

By the time Jamal was in middle school, I didn't know what the hell had gotten into that boy's head. I came home from an out-of-town gig and found him standing in the kitchen wearing a full-face black ski mask, looking like that rapper Pooh Shiesty. "Son, what the fuck is you wearing?" I asked him. "It's ninety-nine degrees outside. You tryna rob somebody?"

Jamal shrugged. "It's hard out here in the hood."

"What 'hood' is you talking about? You got a bidet in your bathroom."

My nephew was having a Black-boy-with-benefits identity crisis, trying to act like he was all about that Pooh Shiesty lifestyle when really he was living like Lionel Richie. It made no damn sense to me.

I've moved through about half a dozen different tax brackets in my lifetime. But there will always be part of me that only sees things from the perspective of that hungry little girl who had nothing and nobody to count on. My messed-up childhood follows me around like a ghost.

It's why I stay hustling and why I never feel financially secure no matter how much money I make. It's why I find it hard to trust folks who treat me nice and why my heart still breaks every time I see a little girl who reminds me of my past.

In March 2026, just as I was finishing this book, I got a call from a friend in Atlanta that my niece Jonelle's children needed help. Ever since 2017, when Jonelle got locked up for armed robbery, her children had been living with Ruth, a woman I knew from back in the day.

I can't imagine how hard it must have been for Ruth to take care of her own four children along with Jonelle's six. She cared for those babies—including Gracie, who Jonelle gave birth to in prison—for almost a decade. That struggle took its toll on Ruth. On Christmas Eve, 2025, she died from cancer.

After that, I came to learn, Jonelle's kids bounced around between

Ruth's sister, Evie, and Ruth's daughter and son, who were barely old enough to care for themselves. I didn't know how bad things were until the day I got a call from Evie. "I know none of Ruth's kids is gonna ask you for help," Evie said. "But they in a house with no lights or heat. Somebody needs to pay their electric bill. They can't be sitting in that house in the dark and cold."

I paid the eleven-hundred-dollar bill and invited the kids to stay at my place for the weekend. I took them to Old Navy and bought them jeans and T-shirts. At Target, I got socks, underwear, and new bras for the girls. At Foot Locker, I bought them Nikes, Jordans, and Air Force 1s. On Sunday night, they went back home to Decatur, with their brand-new book bags filled with all those clothes. But I knew that wasn't enough.

I was especially worried about Jonelle's youngest children, three girls aged thirteen, eleven, and eight. I knew Ruth's sister and children were doing the best they could. But my own life experience has taught me that young girls need a lot of adult supervision to keep them safe. I worried about predators and molesters. I worried about them falling under the spell of drugs and alcohol, or dropping out of school.

My heart was heavy. I couldn't sleep.

God told me what He wanted me to do. I heard His voice loud and clear: "Girl, I didn't give you this big house with all these extra bedrooms for nothing. Go and get those kids."

I asked Michael what he thought. I was sure he wouldn't be with it. But he surprised the hell outta me. He said that ever since Sweetie came to take her kids away two decades earlier, he'd been wondering if we should have fought harder to keep them. "It's like I been feeling guilty for years," he said. "Maybe taking in Jonelle's kids is a way to make amends."

Still, I was menopausal and middle-aged and busy with my comedy and all my TV shows. I didn't feel ready to raise another set of kids, especially when we had Junebug, Michaela, Jamal, Tay-Tay, D'Sani, and twelve-year-old Shirlene living with us already. So, I kept pushing back, asking God over and over, "With all the people you know, you don't have *nobody* else who can take them?"

God just laughed in my face.

It's been two weeks since we brought Jonelle's three girls to come live with us. Me and Michael filed for permanent custody, enrolled them in school, hired a tutor, and got a nanny to help around the house. I don't know all of what those girls went through before we got them. But at night, the little one gets scared. Gracie will come into my room, whispering, "Aunty Pat, you awake?" then crawl into bed beside me.

I know we're helping those children. But I don't think they know how much they're helping me.

A few days ago, I came home from doing three sold-out shows in St. Louis. I was exhausted and irritable and needed peace and quiet. I went to the kitchen to get myself some water. The girls were there with their four cousins, all seven of them sitting around the family table playing a very loud game of Uno.

I'm from the streets. I'm hard as nails. You won't never catch me crying. But at the sound of all those children laughing their little asses off, I just fell apart. I stood there like some soft-ass suburban mom, silently bawling, with tears rolling down my face.

I've worked damn hard to climb the ladder so I could get my American dream. I have a successful career and all the privileges that come with it. But it's true what they say—money can't buy happiness. For me, it's my husband's love and the sound of children laughing they asses off and having fun at my kitchen table that fill my heart with joy.

I found my happiness, y'all. I hope you find your happiness, too.

ACKNOWLEDGMENTS

Surround yourself with only people who are going to lift you higher.
—Oprah Winfrey

Getting this book together took a whole lot of work. I want to thank all the people who helped make this dream come true.

First and foremost, a big thank-you to God for loaning me an angel, Jeannine Amber, the best Book Lady I've ever worked with. She listened to my stories and helped me figure out what this book was about. Without her, this book would have been just a list of people who get on my damn nerves. Thank you, Jeannine, for all your hard work and dedication and for doing interviews with me while I was shopping at Home Depot, Lowe's, and L.O.S. Liquidation Outlet Store.

Thank you to my family for always holding me down when I was out at the clubs chasing my dream, even when it meant you had to work twice as hard to take care of shit at home. Thank you especially to Garrianna, who was like a second mama to all the kids when I was on the road.

Thank you to the love of my life. I don't know how I got to be so lucky to have you as my husband. You put up with all my bullshit, paid all the bills while we were struggling, and are an excellent dad to all the kids. Baby, you didn't leave when you had the chance. Now you're stuck with me forever, because I won't *never* let you go.

Thank you to my assistant, Jasmine, for always staying one step ahead and keeping me calm in the chaos. You keep my shit in order, get me where I need to go, and help me brainstorm ideas. With all you do, you deserve a big fat raise. Just not today.

Thank you so much to Deon, Chris, Jordan, Vincent, Avery, Kiara, Jasmine, Ashley, Garrett, and Garrianna for filling in all the details I couldn't remember (even though I'm pretty sure some of you made some of that shit up, because there's no way I got into that many fistfights).

To DeRay Davis, Katt Williams, Deon Curry, Chris Spangle, Lee Daniels, Jordan E. Cooper, and Debbie Allen, thank you for being there when I was hustling for stage time, trying to make it in Hollywood, or figuring out how to do a podcast. There were times I didn't know what the hell I was doing. Y'all helped me find my way.

Thank you to my friends Ms. Jeanne, Rotunda, and Tracy—you've been my day ones, and I'll never forget it. You supported me through the hard times. You never judged me. You let me learn from my mistakes. That's real friendship. Some people say they got your back, but y'all actually showed it.

Thank you to my team—Kyle, Megan, Reg, Pam, Reed, and Aaron—for keeping me booked and busy and handling everything behind the scenes.

Thank you to the excellent photographer and videographer Fif Wilson for making me look so good on the cover of this book. (If you're reading this and need a photographer, check out @FifWilson!)

Thank you to Julia Cheiffetz for wanting to do this book in the first place.

To my editors, Nick Ciani and Kate Napolitano, thank you for your support, feedback, and for making sure everything is spelled correctly.

Last but not least, thank you to all my fans. Y'all been rocking with me through everything—the jokes, the stories, and all the wild shit

I said that could have got me canceled. You watched the TV shows, bought tickets to my stand-up, shared my clips online, and told your friends, "You gotta hear this crazy lady." I love making you laugh. I am so damn grateful that of all the things you could be doing, you choose to spend your time with me.

ABOUT THE AUTHOR

Patricia "Ms. Pat" Williams-Lee, "the real hero of sitcom TV" (*HuffPost*), is the creator and star of BET+'s Emmy-nominated hit *The Ms. Pat Show*, based on her riveting memoir, *Rabbit*, the story of an inner-city drug dealer turned suburban mom. One of the country's most exciting stand-ups, Williams-Lee regularly headlines comedy clubs and theaters nationwide. Her signature charisma and candor are featured in Netflix's *Ms. Pat: Y'all Wanna Hear Something Crazy?* and on the top-rated comedy podcast *The Patdown with Ms. Pat*. On her TV court show, *Ms. Pat Settles It*, she trades her mic for a gavel to referee disputes with hilarious results. In her downtime, Ms. Pat invites guests to teach her culinary skills on *Whisking It All with Ms. Pat*, her delightful YouTube cooking show. Ms. Pat lives in Atlanta with her husband and a house full of dependents.

Atria Books, an imprint of Simon & Schuster, fosters an open environment where ideas flourish, bestselling authors soar to new heights, and tomorrow's finest voices are discovered and nurtured. Since its launch in 2002, Atria has published hundreds of bestsellers and extraordinary books, which would not have been possible without the invaluable support and expertise of its team and publishing partners. Thank you to the Atria Books colleagues who collaborated on *Ms. American Dream*, as well as to the hundreds of professionals in the Simon & Schuster advertising, audio, communications, design, ebook, finance, human resources, legal, marketing, operations, production, sales, supply chain, subsidiary rights, and warehouse departments who help Atria bring great books to light.

EDITORIAL
Kate Napolitano
Hannah Frankel

JACKET DESIGN
James Iacobelli

MARKETING
Erin Kibby

MANAGING EDITORIAL
Paige Lytle
Shelby Pumphrey
Sofia Echeverry
Abby Borchers

PRODUCTION
Nancy Tonik
Allison Har-zvi
Polly Watson
Davina Mock-Maniscalco

PUBLICITY
Shida Carr
Molly Burgoyne

PUBLISHING OFFICE
Suzanne Donahue
Dana Trocker
Abby Velasco

SUBSIDIARY RIGHTS
Nicole Bond
Sara Bowne
Rebecca Justiniano
Germanie Louis